Philanthropy and Gerontology

**Recent Titles in
Contributions to the Study of Aging**

Geriatric Medicine in the United States and Great Britain
David K. Carboni

Innovative Aging Programs Abroad: Implications for the United States
Charlotte Nusberg, with Mary Jo Gibson and Sheila Peace

The Extreme Aged in America: A Portrait of an Expanding Population
Ira Rosenwaike, with the assistance of Barbara Logue

Old Age in a Bureaucratic Society: The Elderly, the Experts, and the State in American History
David Van Tassel and Peter N. Stearns, editors

The Aged in Rural America
John A. Krout

Public Policy Opinion and the Elderly, 1952–1978
John E. Tropman

The Mirror of Time: Images of Aging and Dying
Joan M. Boyle and James E. Morriss

North American Elders: United States and Canadian Perspectives
Eloise Rathbone-McCuan and Betty Havens, editors

Hispanic Elderly in Transition: Theory, Research, Policy and Practice
Steven R. Applewhite, editor

Religion, Health, and Aging: A Review and Theoretical Integration
Harold George Koenig, Mona Smiley, and Jo Ann Ploch Gonzales

PHILANTHROPY AND GERONTOLOGY

The Role of American Foundations

Ann H. L. Sontz

Foreword by
M. N. Maxey

CONTRIBUTIONS TO THE STUDY OF AGING, NUMBER 12
Erdman B. Palmore, *Series Adviser*

GREENWOOD PRESS
New York • Westport, Connecticut • London

Library of Congress Cataloging-in-Publication Data

Sontz, Ann H. L.
  Philanthropy and gerontology : the role of American foundations / Ann H. L. Sontz ; foreword by M. N. Maxey.
    p.   cm. — (Contributions to the study of aging, ISSN 0732-085X ; no. 12)
  Bibliography: p.
  Includes index.
  ISBN 0-313-26097-4 (lib. bdg. : alk. paper)
  1. Gerontology—Study and teaching—United States—Finance.
 2. Gerontology—Research—United States—Finance.   3. Endowment of research—United States—History.   4. Endowments—United States—History.   5. Social sciences—Study and teaching—United States—Finance—History.   6. Social sciences—Research—United States—Finance—History.   7. Gerontology—Research—United States—History—Statistics.   I. Title.   II. Series.
HQ1064.U5S5985   1989
305.2'6'072—dc 19   89-1679

British Library Cataloguing in Publication Data is available.

Copyright © 1989 by Ann H. L. Sontz

All rights reserved. No portion of this book may be reproduced, by any process or technique, without the express written consent of the publisher.

Library of Congress Catalog Card Number: 89-1679
ISBN: 0-313-26097-4
ISSN: 0732-085X

First published in 1989

Greenwood Press, Inc.
88 Post Road West, Westport, Connecticut 06881

Printed in the United States of America

The paper used in this book complies with the Permanent Paper Standard issued by the National Information Standards Organization (Z39.48-1984).

10 9 8 7 6 5 4 3 2 1

For Howard and David-Benjamin

Among the first groups of beings with whom men must have made contracts were the spirits of the dead . . . with whom it was particularly necessary to exchange and particularly dangerous not to; but on the other hand, with them exchange was the easiest and fastest.

Marcel Mauss, 1923

> Wrapt into future times I . . .
> See from this charitable plan,
> The youth by learning form'd to man,
> And fitted to the skies.

Charles Churchill, 1767

Contents

Exhibits	*xi*
Foreword	*xv*
Preface and Acknowledgments	*xvii*
Introduction: Charity for the Few, for the Many	*xix*
1. A Mistrust of Trusts: Early Benefactions to Science	1
2. Kin and Nonkin: The Gradual Life Cycle of Early Foundations	17
3. Charity, Sociology, Ethnography	35
4. The Unreclaimed Land: Social Gerontology as Area Study	49
5. Entering the Aging Mode: Social Gerontology and the Universities	73
6. The Calculus of Charity: Funding for Social Gerontology	89

x   CONTENTS

7. Facing Age Neutrally   107
APPENDIX: National Foundations Giving Grants to
          Social Gerontology Research   123
Selected Bibliography   *125*
Index   *131*

Exhibits

2.1	Selected Early Foundations	19
2.2	Age, Occupational, Relational, and Board Distribution of Trustees of Five Major Foundations at Period of Start-up and 1970	22
2.3	Affiliations of Individual Research Grants at Seventy-seven Large Foundations, 1953	25
2.4	Areas of Foundation Activity, 1968	26
4.1	Employed Male Population in 1900, by Occupational Sector, Origin, and Ethnicity	54
4.2	Proportion of Adults over Sixty-five Years to the General U.S. Population, by Sex and Decade, 1890–1920	55
4.3	Percentage in Population of Adults over Sixty-five in Selected Countries, 1926	55
4.4	Area Study Gerontology in the Social Sciences: Ph.D. Productivity by Year, 1934–1966	59
4.5	Ph.D. Productivity in Aging Studies at Selected Universities by Total Number of Dissertations, 1934–1969	60

4.6	Area Study Gerontology Ph.D.s in Anthropology, Sociology, and Social Work as a Proportion of Disciplinary Ph.D.s, 1963–1985	61
4.7	Area Study Gerontology Ph.D.s as a Proportion of All Anthropology, Sociology, and Social Work Doctorates, 1963–1985, by Time Period	62
4.8	Doctoral Productivity in Anthropology, Sociology, and Social Work, 1963–1985	63
4.9	Social Gerontology Ph.D.-Producing Universities as a Proportion of All Doctoral Producers, by Year	64
4.10	Selected Universities as Significant Social Gerontology Ph.D. Producers, 1963–1985	65
4.11	Percentage Distribution of Significant Social Gerontology Theses Topics, by Discipline, 1963–1985	68
4.12	Representation of Minority, Ethnic, and Cross-Cultural Studies in Area-Focus Gerontology Ph.D.s, by Academic Discipline, 1963–1985	70
5.1	Percentage of Gerontology-Area-Focus Ph.D.s Pursuing Aging Research at Postdoctoral Level, by Discipline, 1963–1985	75
5.2	Proportion Gerontology-Area-Focus Ph.D.s, 1963–1985, by Postdoctoral Gerontology Productivity and Employment Sphere	76
5.3	Distribution of Doctoral and Postdoctoral Research Topics in Social Gerontology, 1963–1985	77
5.4	Funding Sources of Ph.D. Theses in Social Gerontology, 1963–1985	78
5.5	Postdoctoral Aging Research Funding in Anthropology, Sociology, and Social Work, 1963–1985	78
5.6	Academic or Organizational Units of Gerontology Instruction, 1986	80
5.7	Type of Degree and Credentialing in Gerontology on American Campuses, 1986	81

5.8	Percentage Representation of Disciplinary Course Work in Undergraduate Gerontology Programs, 1985	82
5.9	Percentage Representation of Disciplinary Course Work in Graduate Gerontology Programs, 1985	83
6.1	Grant Distribution of NIA to Selected Areas in Gerontology, 1978 and 1984	91
6.2	Grants for Selected Population Groups by 444 Foundations, 1981 and 1985	93
6.3	Foundation Grant Making for Aging Projects and Research, by Foundation Type, 1976 and 1985	94
6.4	Selected Foundation Giving to Aging Programs and Aging Research, by Foundation Type, 1984–1986	95
6.5	Foundation Supports to Programs for the Elderly by Focus of Support, 1984	96
6.6	Funding Sources of Published Social Gerontology Studies, 1976–1986	97
6.7	Funding Agencies by Type: Single-Source Grants for Published Articles, 1976–1986	98
6.8	Subject Matter of Published Articles in Social Gerontology, 1976–1986	99
6.9	Project Methods in Social Gerontology, by Participating Funding Agents, 1976–1986	100
6.10	Type of Postdoctoral Social Gerontology Projects Anticipated, by Methodology and Estimated Cost	102

Foreword

Ann Sontz elevates our understanding of responsibility to new horizons in this careful study of the needs of an aging population and the unique virtues of philanthropic foundations in responding to these needs.
  She clearly recognizes three stubborn matters of fact. First, the proportion of older adults in America has not only increased dramatically since 1900 but will increase steadily to 20 percent of the population early in the next century. Second, although massive federal bureaucracies are able to pour much more money into medical research than can private foundations, the glacial speed with which they can be responsive to rapidly changing human needs exacerbates the unfortunate fact that the aging are viewed primarily, if not exclusively, as a medical problem rather than a social and cultural challenge. Third, besides a medicalization of problems posed by an aging population, their segregation and isolation as yet another minority subject to philanthropic largesse can only result in further fragmentation of our social fabric.
  Confronted with these challenges, Dr. Sontz asks her readers to recall the impressive history of America's pioneering private

foundations: Rockefeller, Russell Sage, Carnegie Corporation, Milbank Memorial Fund, and others. Although endowments for scientific research during the nineteenth century were episodic, this changed as needs of the twentieth century were quickly recognized. Just as private foundations once supported the process of discipline building in the social sciences and social work earlier in this century, Dr. Sontz recommends that they now support the development of social and cultural gerontology research in contemporary university systems. She expresses confidence that by refocusing and reformulating problems posed by an aging population, graduate medical schools can be relied upon to recognize the necessity for more holistic treatment and to emulate university curricula by enriching courses in geriatrics with social and cultural studies.

Dr. Sontz applauds the fact that corporate foundations have already responded to problems of isolation by including older, experienced, and mature workers in the labor force; by supporting trusts for senior centers; by reinforcing a standardization of biomedical research, diagnosis, and treatment. Nonetheless, the genius of the private philanthropic foundation—the capacity and flexibility to shift priorities quickly, giving researchers latitude for innovation—remains more an auspicious promise than a widely acclaimed achievement.

The era of omnicompetent government never was and never will be, and the private foundation attests to an incontrovertible reality of life. As founding president of a private foundation, the Brunswick Institute, Ann Sontz has not only distinguished herself in human development studies but has also demonstrated the ultimate purpose of the art of teaching: to translate theory into practice.

M. N. Maxey, Ph.D.
Professor, Biomedical Engineering Program
University of Texas at Austin

Preface and Acknowledgments

It is widely believed that philanthropic foundations have enjoyed a freedom and flexibility of action largely unfamiliar to public granting agencies. Private endowments established with an eye toward perpetual administration seem to possess a latitude public entities lack for undertaking substantial risks in supporting innovative scientific and program-linked endeavors. On the one hand, foundations are removed from the restraints surrounding legislative appropriations and their scheduling. On the other, they are conceptually isolated from the more direct pressures of interest groups with diverse and competing claims on foundation grant making.

This small inquiry into foundation activity has been channeled in a limited direction. The growth of older adults in our population has been dramatic over the past fifty years. Therefore I have asked how foundation support has mediated the research options of an increasing number of scholars who focus on the social and cultural organization of aging and of the aging process. An additional and related query has focused on the influence of selected private foundations on the entry of researchers into gerontological studies, as well as on their interests and methodological approaches.

Simply to state such a program is perhaps to skirt a complexity rather than to confront it in any satisfactory way. Yet this program builds on an established view of foundations as integral parts of an institutional context in which emergent scientific ideas take on significant professional roots. Such a program has also implied a need to marshal helpful resources from a variety of quarters. I am indebted to personally unknown scholars of philanthropy as well as to others who have generously shared with me their knowledge of charity history. Laura Robbins of the John A. Hartford Foundation gave me suggestions regarding an examination of the informal texture of foundation life. While they were at the Ford Foundation, Dr. Elinor Barber and Dr. Warren Ilchman undertook a review of doctoral production in International Studies. This review served as a highly useful model of the growth of social gerontology, another interdisciplinary field as yet of smaller scope and penetration in the academic marketplace. I also thank Dr. Anthony Glascock and Dr. Barbara Hornum of Drexel University and Dr. Nancy J. Osgood of the Virginia Commonwealth University for their insights and encouragement.

Dr. James Birren, Brookdale Distinguished Scholar at the Andrus Gerontology Center, was kind enough to articulate for me in correspondence the continuing medicalization of aging research. Dr. Edward Masaro, University of Texas at San Antonio, brings great enthusiasm to the study of the biology of the aging process. His interest in a book on social gerontology was invaluable.

Many others have contributed special supportive energies to this project. I single out Gillian Crosby, assistant director of the Centre for Policy on Ageing in London, and Joseph Cornwall, president of the Fund for New Jersey, for their help in locating source materials and in understanding foundation finances. Sharon Tucker of the Jersey City library was most kind in tracking down archival materials I would not have been able to obtain so easily. Professor Paula Rubel and Professor Abraham Rosman of the Department of Anthropology, Columbia University, always deserve continuing gratitude. I hope they will recognize the legitimacy of a need for a slightly different trajectory from the one along which I began.

Introduction: Charity for the Few, for the Many

The history of endowed foundations is a long and distinguished one yet appears regularly clustered in civilizations where economic and urban growth has been fruitful for some but not for the many. The ancient Greeks and Romans supported a flourishing foundation life. The philanthropic quest there, however, was less socially ameliorative than supportive of the civic and the cultural. Modern foundations, in contrast, have been reformist in charter and have found among the indigent and the dislocated a charitable territory unrecognized by the classical organizations.

It cannot be said that the great centuries separating the ancient and contemporary foundations were philanthropically vague or empty. Indeed the extensive Tudor and Stuart charities, as well as the nineteenth-century Charity Organization Movement in England and America, provided urban poverty continuing largesse. Nonetheless, for a lengthy period in history, charitable giving maintained a distinctly individualistic character. Even at its most eminent in design and sponsorship, therefore, early philanthrophy still seems undirected and haphazard given the vast burdens it sought to relieve.

The trend across these many years has been away from individual benefactions toward the enclosure of the charitable impulse within endowed foundations. Though charitable donations by individuals remain plentiful, they have been decisively supplemented by institutionalized grant giving. The philanthropic mandate of the modern foundations continues to encompass the support of programs that aid the poor and the socially vulnerable. In addition, the twentieth century has seen the channeling of vast philanthropic resources to scientific and social scientific endeavors that justify and guide foundation activities.

This book claims a small parcel of terrain within the modern foundation for the purpose of review and assessment. It focuses on that aspect of foundation life that links foundation grant giving with social science insofar as that science is concerned with the elderly and with studies of later life. Modern foundations are themselves not of great age. The majority of the largest and most well-known endowments, the Carnegie, Rockefeller, and Russell Sage foundations, arose only as a result of wealth accumulated in the late nineteenth and early twentieth centuries. Moreover, foundations, unlike individual benefactors, do not anticipate finality but rather are designed for perpetual existence. If this staying power has not always been evident, it has been remarkably pervasive within the charitable community. Given the extensive growth of our older adult population and the expansion of gerontology studies within the social sciences, it seems appropriate to question how foundations have responded to the challenges of our aging society. Such an inquiry takes on increased significance in the light of the traditional foundation mandate for social reform and a pronounced interest in the sponsorship of interdisciplinary approaches within the social sciences that can increase the effectiveness of foundation programming.

Much of the relevant commentary on modern private foundations has stressed their smaller stature in comparison to the grant-making potential of burgeoning federal bureaucracies. As early as the 1960s, one distinguished student of charity history, David Owen, was prompted to call foundations the "junior partner in the welfare firm" (Owen, 1964:527). Alongside this negative emphasis, however, has come the belief that the financial independence of philanthropic foundations allows them to activate their particular mandate in a risk-taking way. In large measure, this creativity has been ample as in the path-breaking work of Rockefeller Foundation subventions to psychiatric medicine in the 1930s. A review of the more contemporary evidence nevertheless indicates no such formative response to the elderly or to associated social gerontological studies. What response there has been appears to be of the great foundations acting as sustaining institutions, not as innovating ones.

An intense public awareness that our older adult population is growing rapidly forms a crucial part of the background for this study. Interest groups and debates over rising health costs have also provoked public concern. Striking shifts in our demography have been the subject of media attention as well, so that relevant data on the elderly have reached a broad and growing audience. The statistics are the stuff of descriptive journalism yet warrant restatement. Between 1900 and the early 1980s, the proportion of those sixty-five years of age or older in American society trebled. This growth represented an actual quantitative expansion of just over 3 million, to almost 27.4 million people. Average life expectancies have now passed seventy-four years, while those over eighty-five years of age, the oldest old, also expanded numerically. Today these number 2.5 million persons, a figure twenty-five times larger than that of a century ago. Demographers seem certain that the proportion of older adults in the population will increase at a relatively steady pace well into the next century. By the year 2000, those over sixty-five years will constitute at least 13 percent of the population. This proportion will reach, or exceed, 21 percent by that century's third decade.

There seem few aspects of society that such a demographic shift will not touch. Among these are changes in the strength and quality of intergenerational ties, labor force participation rates, and scope of health care interventions. The question of how to retain the talents and experiences of the mature while at the same time permitting more youthful members of society to gain access to positions of power and prestige looms increasingly large on the sociological and political horizon. The concept of a "third age" and the options and conflicts accompanying it is quickly becoming fashionable. As one recent report put it, "It scarcely makes sense for us as a society to spend one-third of our life preparing for work and another third in retirement from it" (Nee and Bracco, 1986:73).

Along with increased public awareness of our aging population, many academic disciplines have begun to encounter the relatively new common frontier of aging studies through their own disciplinary perspectives. The contributions of biogerontology, the study of the biological bases of aging, are clarifying questions concerning human life expectancies and age-linked deteriorations as distinct from those related to disease or lifestyle. Psychogerontology has focused on personality and cognition among the aged, as well as on a range of issues surrounding the definition of what is normal, "successful," or pathological with respect to elderly individuals and to older adults as a group. Social gerontology, within which I include both the data and theoretical approaches found in anthropology, sociology, and social work, is one of the most well-established fields in late-age studies. Its perspective concentrates largely on understanding the role of social and cultural forces in mediating the biologically based processes of aging and in influencing individual and group adjustment to later life.

Federal funding has tended to favor psychogerontology and biomedically oriented studies of later life. Modern foundations would therefore seem to have an innovative entry point into aging studies in the form of social gerontology research supports. One result of such subventions would be an increasingly sophisticated knowledge base, which could aid medical compliance and illness prevention among older adults and help to assess prevalent myths about aging that leave the elderly incompletely integrated into society.

Philanthropic foundations and academic social gerontology do not yet share rich relations. The bond between the two nevertheless becomes more evident when viewed from an understanding of foundation influence on the growth of anthropology, sociology, and social work in American institutions of higher learning. By utilizing a historical perspective, the catalytic role of foundations in social science development can be reclaimed in order to clarify the ways in which social gerontology can be effectively included in a contemporary philanthropic agenda. The current paucity of foundation funding for social gerontology can also be linked to past population trends and contexts. We may thus avoid indulging in the overly critical custom of calling foundation billions "timid" whenever grant-making directions fail to conform to individual needs or expectations.

This study has not sought to address the character of foundation work relative to elderly individuals. Indeed, recent years have witnessed a definite gain in foundation grant making for retirement community financing, senior centers, nursing homes, and home health services. The social and cultural sciences that inform treatment and service delivery among the elderly, however, still remain at the fringe of organized philanthropy. This distance from the center of foundation work stands in contrast to the early days of foundation development, which provide a vivid picture of subventions that underwrote the growth of university systems and a range of ventures that ultimately crafted social research and theory in a lasting way.

If foundations today can claim only a minor role in social gerontology growth because of the primacy of federal grant making, I would still not exclude them from what Bernard Barber (1952) termed the dominant research triangle of individual, university, and government. One reason is that social gerontology is a new subfield within the social sciences. Relevant federal funding agencies are also emergent and relatively undercapitalized given rising research demands. Another reason is that the equation of size of assets with institutional potential for provoking creative research responses does not seem to fit the historical profile of a pronounced foundation talent for identifying areas of interest left unexamined by overachieving bureaucracies. Productivity measured in quantities has little significant tie to additions to current knowledge, and even a latter-day admirer of the famed Lowell Institute in Massachusetts seriously questioned whether a growing endowment had produced any more wisdom than the institute's earliest, more financially meager phases (Weeks, 1966).

Still another reason not to push foundation monies prematurely to the periphery of involvement in social gerontology research is the current institutional character of federal grant making. Government grants for aging studies stem largely from the National Institute on Aging, a rather recent addition to the scientific scene and one that retains a prominent biomedical orientation. Core disciplines within social gerontology, such as anthropology, actually receive the bulk of their support from the National Science Foundation. Since peer review committees differ from agency to agency, emergent trends in anthropological gerontology can be overlooked or neglected. While it seems that scholarship in social gerontology will continue to be dependent on public monies in the future, foundations may offer a welcome funding alternative and help to compensate for a continuing federal emphasis on the biomedical and biological components of aging research.

Finally, although monies from philanthropic foundations have not as yet rewarded research potential in social gerontology, they have supported a variety of projects concerned with health service delivery to the elderly. These programs have enlarged the spectrum of clinical practice and fostered the growth of interdisciplinary applications in practice settings. There are few fields other than gerontology that are in a position to draw so heavily on the social and cultural sciences in clinical environments in order to evolve differential diagnoses and treatment plans for elders of varied ethnic backgrounds. Foundation grant making for social gerontology could be rather easily tied to its own project base and to issues of health intervention without necessarily raising limited budgets too greatly or reorienting program priorities.

This book offers an evaluation of the contributions of modern foundations to the growth of social science earlier in the twentieth century. It also outlines a few of the ways in which a knowledge of these contributions can influence the growth of foundation work relative to social gerontology today. I have therefore reasserted the belief that science itself remains both a legitimate object of philanthropy as well as an accepted subject of charity history. The first three chapters summarize the evolution of major American foundations and their impact on the academic expansion of anthropology, sociology, and social work. Chapter 4 deals with the growth of late-age studies in these disciplines as measured by trends in Ph.D. productivity and by the increased inclusion of social gerontology course work into curriculum planning in higher education. The fifth and sixth chapters clarify current foundation grant making for late-age studies in the light of a sample survey of social gerontology scholars, their research plans, and associated funding requirements. The concluding chapter suggests a series of niches within contemporary social gerontology that might be particularly amenable to foundation support.

I acknowledge here some of my prejudices gained before this book was written and during its preparation. I have written largely for foundation officials and for those interested in foundation life. Those more enmeshed in the academy might balk at the inclusion of social work in a social science category. However, as an administrator of a nonprofit research institute, I have become sensitive to the many sociology projects conducted in tandem with research social workers. Social work has its predominating clinical side. For many decades now, however, the production of doctoral dissertations in that field with late age as a focus has outpaced the growth of gerontology theses in anthropology and sociology. Moreover, social workers with a gerontology specialization are increasingly prized in university research and teaching positions.

As a cultural anthropologist, I have perhaps placed too much emphasis on the formative phase of American culturological studies and may thus have bypassed the efforts of physical anthropology or human biology. An aging focus within physical anthropology, however, is still in an incipient stage. Physical anthropological studies of the aging process remain less developed in quantity, though not in quality, than those of anthropological gerontology, which can trace its intellectual origins to work carried out in the 1940s. Here I indicate how foundation grants to cultural anthropology molded early scholarly responses to data collection and interpretation. Foundation ties to emergent sociology and social work are also highlighted, while the role of philanthropic trusts in fostering departmental specialization within the social sciences is sketched in miniature without developing this complex process into another needed book.

Psychogerontology is not considered in this discussion, and not only because it lies outside my own province. Though less favored than biomedical research on aging in government circles, psychogerontology has nevertheless received more federal funding attention than social gerontology.[1] Moreover, foundation grant making to psychological research has itself been traditionally restricted by the interest of the philanthropic trusts in aiding populations in economic need and in promoting social welfare among particular ethnic and lower-income groups. This book addresses that aspect of late-age studies that comprehends both cross-cultural and cross-national viewpoints. It is this type of research that can help us confront what is universal to the aging process and that which has been considerably molded by culture and context. When the aging process is seen as largely devoid of its current negative stereotypes, we will ultimately be able to encounter, in Jennie Keith's words, "old people as people" (Keith, 1982).

I can write at the outset that foundation giving to the sociocultural study of aging has been constrained and episodic. This pattern of intermittent funding appears to mirror that of an earlier period in the relationship between philanthropy and scientific activity, the nineteenth-century era of piecemeal science patronage described in Chapter 1. It would be difficult to deny that the episodic nature of foundation grants to social gerontology persists despite significant increases in our older adult population and the strengthening bond between social gerontology research and instruction in university systems. It is arguable, however, that clarified intellectual growth can long proceed fruitfully in a relative funding vacuum. If the potential resources are sizable, the actual extent of foundation involvement in social gerontology has been narrow, pragmatic, and unwedded to theoretical and higher educational developments in the field. In the early decades of the century, even limited federal support for science was regarded by many eminent observers as an unwarranted intrusion in the life of the emergent scientific community (Kevles, 1987:152). Science patronage on the part of the major foundations grew grudgingly but accommodatingly into a widening yet seemingly vacant philanthropic niche. Today, though the size and scope of federal grant-making powers have become accepted, these powers remain only loosely attached to aging research in the social sciences. American foundations are therefore in a favorable position to undertake a creative and risk-taking role once again. This role needs to be assumed not only for the sake of social reform or social welfare causes but also as an enlightened response to a rising demographic imperative.

NOTE

1. Foundation funding to biogerontology is discussed along with a consideration of grant making to aging research in medicine in Chapters 5 and 6.

1

A Mistrust of Trusts:
Early Benefactions to Science

> Pending that millennium [systematic assistance for science] we must wrestle with the generous and the wealthy.
> George Davidson, 1892[1]

The onset of the twentieth century was a frustrating time for scientists like George Davidson, an astronomer and former president of the California Academy of Sciences. A growing number of technically proficient people had been searching for the type of sustained fiscal support needed for geological surveys, scientific instrumentation, and academic endowments for laboratories and professional salaries. For the greater part of the nineteenth century, however, patronage to science depended largely on the ability of the individual researcher in emergent institutions to engage in successful negotiations with wealthy benefactors (Miller, 1970:48).[2] To the extent that salesmanship proved fruitful, its results moved the contemporary scientific enterprise to the point where it could attract reigning European personalities such as the renowned naturalist Louis Agassiz, who delivered the Lowell Lectures in Boston and later remained at Harvard's Lawrence Scientific School (Miller, 1970:51).

The personal factor in science patronage nevertheless suggested that disparities in the social status of wealthy benefactor and needy scientist might intrude in the grant-giving process. Frequently their transactions were marked by a failure to marshall resources to a worthy scientific cause. Just as frequently, the lone scientist was forced to adjust research goals to the eccentricities of a particular donor. While it was true that nineteenth-century scientists found themselves increasingly grouped into associations, among them the American Association for the Advancement of Science, the contemporary philanthropic community still lacked extensive permanent endowments or grant making guided by professionals. Although nineteenth-century science benefactions were ad hoc and contingent, their interpersonal aura occasionally left the individual investigator considerable room for maneuver. Scientists were relatively unbothered by persistent institutional inertia; their "fields of action extended to the limits of their patrons' vision and their promoters' zeal" (Miller, 1970:97).

This piecemeal patronage to science is linked to the legal and philosophical limitations on charitable incorporation that permeated much of the nineteenth century. Endowments for public purposes were not actually unaccepted in early America and indeed dominated over the paucity of private charity. Ambivalent attitudes still persisted unless trusts were properly bonded to public goals. So bonded, the "oppressive" nature of incorporation could be dampened. As the historian Peter Dobkin Hall has noted, "Incorporation was not necessarily viewed as granting monopoly privileges the right of perpetual succession, or immunity from legislative accountability" (Hall, 1984:97).

The selective scope of trust and corporate tolerance was also prominent in the first decades of the nineteenth century. Political democracy had expanded; much debate centered around how to maintain a balance between private interest and public control. In New England the equity power of the courts grew gradually, and in that region the integrity of capital endowed for charitable and educational purposes was retained without restrictive state intrusions. In the mid-Atlantic states, in contrast, the climate toward private endowments remained unsupportive. Amounts left to estates were constrained by the legislatures. After the 1820s, further constraints on trust development arose because of limitations on property gifts to incorporated institutions.

The mistrust of trusts manifested itself in predictable ways. If endowments could be rather freely generated in New England, then indigenous educational institutions, such as Yale and Harvard, benefited. Harvard, for example, received nearly $1.5 million between 1800 and mid-century. Columbia University in New York accepted benefactions of only $30,000 during that time. While New England's cultural and educational life flourished, New York, the great Hudson entry port, had few institutions that were targets of the grand charitable impulse (Hall, 1984:122). Statutes there changed only in the late nineteenth century after a justifiable public outcry when the city was forced to turn down a $5 million bequest for the construction of a major library. Subsequently previously neglected Gotham grew into a towering cultural capital, as well as the center of foundation life; venerable Columbia University received $8 million in welcome gifts in the short seven years before 1900 (Hall, 1984: 123).

Besides selective educational and cultural development, another outcome of the mistrust of charitable trusts during the nineteenth century was that institutional growth in American charity history tended toward the public in character. New York assumed a relative preeminence in charitable institutions for the mentally disordered and the indigent. Elsewhere, where the legal basis for eleemosynary trusts was similarly underprivileged, local communities and state legislatures channeled funds into asylums for the poor and the aged. Private donations on the part of individuals also played an integral role in nineteenth-century charity and lay behind the growth of benevolent associations that responded to severe population dislocations following the Civil War and to the onset of massive immigration from Europe. In metropolitan locations, these associations were often ethnically based and without sustaining endowments. Poor financial conditions in the late nineteenth century, however, dampened the probability that immigrants of some fiscal means or savings would continue associational gift giving on anything but an episodic basis. Charitable donations to the ethnic poor thus came increasingly from indigenous middle-income Americans. "Friendly visitors" attached to charity organization societies contacted the neighborhood indigent and aged personally but also gave extensive benefactions to these societies' efforts to coordinate metropolitan philanthropy.

The work and benefactions of the friendly visitors continued on into the early twentieth century just as private donations to charity societies grew more widespread in the middle-class public and through community chests. Patron volunteerism gradually declined in favor of the scientific philanthropist—the social worker with a professional self who was guided by a specialized university education and system of diagnosis and treatment (Lubove, 1974). Sustaining and systematic endowments to social work education and related social welfare research did not, however, find a lasting basis until the second decade of the twentieth century with the advent of formative grant making on the part of a select number of newly established private philanthropic foundations.

Negative attitudes toward eleemosynary trusts also mediated patronage to science and science education during much of the last century. An intermittent pattern of giving broadly paralleled episodic benefactions to social welfare causes. Although the notable missionizing aspect attached to friendly visiting was relatively absent on the part of donors, the growth of the American scientific community became linked to an expanding patriotic zeal, or more specifically to that part of patriotism tied to equaling, if not surpassing, European scientific achievements. For charity volunteers, monetary gifts combined with local visiting encompassed both a form of noblesse oblige and a sense of self-fulfillment over "client" improvements. The growing attachment of science patronage to patriotic ideals, however, made donor rewards for benefactions to science seem contrastive. For example, to write that nineteenth-century American scientists were merely in need of subventions from wealthier quarters is to understate the contemporary view of a more dire state of impoverishment (Miller, 1970:3, 8). A definite threshold in science patronage was reached only in 1846 when the trust of the English chemist James Smithson was activated and the Smithsonian Institution in Washington finally launched. The link of science to a permanent home in the national capital helped endow investigators in geology, astronomy, and the natural sciences with a positive place in the American cultural hierarchy; science benefactions could therefore evolve under the halo effect of the Smithsonian. Personal benevolence to the needy tended to reaffirm an individual's growing wealth and concern for the indigent. Science patronage offered the wealthy donor an even more prestigious way of transforming an elevated economic status into a position replete with national attention and recognition.

It is necessary to note that although patronage to nineteenth-century science remained private and episodic, donations were becoming increasingly directed toward specialists in institutional contexts. Astronomical observatories formed only one fertile field of interest for the wealthy patron and the smaller donor alike. Appropriate instrumentation loomed continually large in the astronomer's tool kit and was best found imported and of costly European invention. So challenged, the trustees of Williams College contributed to the cost of a college observatory in 1838; in the 1840s observatories at Harvard and at Cincinnati were established with private patronage from wealthy businessmen and with subscriptions from the general public (Miller, 1970:36). Lack of permanent endowments at Cincinnati, however, stymied research efforts. At Harvard, in contrast, the regional mercantile class helped purchase more technical apparatus and provided funds for professorial salaries. Miller's well-drawn documentation of nineteenth-century science patronage notes that one of Harvard's largest benefactions originated in the largesse of Edward Phillips, the son of a church deacon. Phillips's youthful friendship with a student astronomer eventually produced a $100,000 gift to the college for research and for scientists' salaries (Miller, 1970:38). Besides adding to the coffers of the prestigious institution, this gift also highlighted how a historical acceptance of trusts had benefited New England's continuing educational and cultural influence.

With passing time, accompanied by the strikingly visible astronomical attractions of the century, private philanthropy followed on the personal appeals of a small number of scientists and on public enthusiasm. Though it favored regions without negative attitudes toward trusts and incorporation, piecemeal patronage solidified the link between astronomy and a westwardly expanding higher education system. Nevertheless, despite public recognition and scientific patronage on the part of wealthy American benefactors, the center of scientific gravity clung steadfastly to European soil well into the first few decades of the twentieth century.

Astronomy was not the only science in nineteenth-century America that had to wrestle with the wealthy for admittedly generous, if intermittent, funding. The fiscal attention of the mercantile classes was hard won. Such attention, once courted, sometimes declined disappointingly after lengthy suits of favor on behalf of natural science projects as well as emergent sociological research. When even the much respected Agassiz failed to win a single efficient source of support for a critical multivolume work on the natural history of North America, his sole resource came in the form of book subscriptions peddled to the general public (Miller, 1970:52–53).

Asa Gray, an eminent botanist and Harvard colleague of Agassiz, repeatedly had to adapt his desires for a national botanical center and laboratory to the predilections of a potential donor. Henry Shaw was a wealthy English merchant who had transplanted himself successfully to St. Louis, increased his fortune in real estate dealings, and energetically set about to erect a botanical garden similar to that of the Kew in London. It took Gray an equal amount of energy to convince the English expatriate that the St. Louis botanical gardens should also contain a scientific research facility. Just as Shaw was prepared to endow the scientific center, a breach-of-promise suit brought by one of his female companions tied up the necessary capital for a critical number of years. Eventually the beleaguered benefactor thoughtfully transferred to Washington University a hefty sum for a School of Botany and for an endowed Asa Gray Professorship. These gifts, however, occurred only upon Shaw's own death and just eighteen months before Gray himself passed away (Miller, 1970:62–65).

EARLY BENEFACTIONS TO SCIENCE 7

The fund-raising expertise of Harvard's Agassiz had succeeded through public appeals and book subscriptions when a choice individual benefactor failed to appear. A similar technique was resurrected at Yale during the course of supplementing Joseph Sheffield's repeated donations for a scientific and agricultural school. With poor financial conditions besetting the nation in the late 1850s, Yale hired a recent graduate, Daniel Coit Gilman, to coordinate the school's public relations and advertising (Barber, 1952:159). Gilman proved an exceedingly competent and distinguished man whose early experiences in philanthropic management and higher education took him to the presidency of the Carnegie Institution in Washington in 1904. Prior to that post, he had held the presidency of the newly opened Johns Hopkins University, where he acquired an interest in social welfare concerns; a presidency of the Conference on Charities and Correction followed (Donaldson, 1904; Flexner, 1915a). It was at the Carnegie Institution, founded in 1902, that biological research, together with scientific investigations in economics, sociology, and anthropology, first received both sustained foundation interest and departmental specialization (Donaldson, 1904:1013).

W. I. Thomas, the Chicago University sociologist, did not fare as well as Asa Gray while attempting to put sociological research on a firm footing. Thomas had appealed to Helen Culver, an astute businesswoman and patron of Jane Addams's Hull House, which was named for Culver's first cousin, real estate magnate Charles J. Hull (Miller, 1970:159-162). At first, Culver appeared set on leaving her entire fortune to a niece who, prematurely it turned out, had promised Professor Thomas an endowment for the newly opened sociology department at Chicago. After three years of negotiations with university personnel, however, Culver appeared to bypass her niece, sociology, and what she termed the "arts" and turned toward a healthy gift to the university's natural sciences and anatomy departments instead. The endowment process, officially completed in 1987, built solidly on a previous course of science giving by other Chicago philanthropists. On this list stood Sidney Kent, whose $150,000 donation underwrote a chemistry laboratory, and Martin Ryerson, a university trustee, who had matched Kent's amount and donated heavily to a laboratory devoted to physics

(Miller, 1970:158). Ryerson's gift came just at the historical moment when Cornell, an eastern university, seemed to be outpacing other university representatives in the leading physics journal. It is also likely that both Kent and Ryerson were aware that a much respected Clark University professor, Arthur Gordon Webster, continued to refer sarcastically to the American scientific enterprise as "painfully small" (Kevles, 1987:76).

The absence of substantial research endowments at Chicago constrained the fiscal supports though not the influential quality of urban sociology at that institution in the decades to follow. Much of the brilliant empirical work on urban demographics and on the linkages among delinquency, poverty, and health status complemented the social worker's need to tie environmental understandings to "social diagnosis" and treatment. This early sociology was conducted within the city of Chicago itself, a fact that considerably defrayed travel costs to distant points. Funding for sociological research at Chicago University emanated largely from the purses and pants' pockets of professor and graduate student alike. Even Nels Anderson's classic study, *The Hobo*, was produced as late as the 1920s for a total sum of $300 (Burgess and Bogue, 1964:6).

Intermittent endowments for the natural and physical sciences, however, eventually bore their own impressive fruit. Although his formative work had been carried out at a series of other institutions, A. A. Michelson, head professor of physics at Chicago's new Ryerson Laboratory, came through with the country's first Nobel Prize in 1907 (Miller, 1970:158). The aura surrounding Michelson's internationally recognized achievements safely hovered over the University of Chicago, as well as around the nascent physics community in additional institutions of higher learning. Ultimately such an achievement spurred popular encouragement for science and helped generate increased funding commitments for physics and for scientific activity in other academic fields as well (Kevles, 1987:79).

Similar to early sociology, emergent anthropology suffered from a lack of sustenance for research. This lack of support was particularly evident before the 1920s and the onset of public and private funding. Urban sociology at Chicago literally demanded studies of the social and cultural fabric of city life. These were ultimately designed to inform far less empirical grand social theorems that had predominated in the past century. In a similar vein, the quest of the early anthropologists was to get out of the academic armchair in order to replace the speculations of cultural evolutionary theory with actual data on traditional lifeways. Amerindian field sites were, however, decidedly removed from the universities and anthropological museums of the East Coast. Nevertheless, the changes advancing Western civilization had brought to traditional societies were seen as trenchantly affecting their ways of life. These rapidly occurring changes made it a pressing responsibility to mount efficient expeditions in order to "salvage" the remains of indigenous cultures before they "disappeared." Self-financed research was nonetheless not an alternative funding source for anthropologists, at least not in the way it had been among Chicago's sociologists with their close-to-home studies and partial ethnographies.

The experiences of Franz Boas, the patriarch of American anthropology and founder of its first academic department at Columbia University in 1899, illustrate the contemporary paucity of consistent funding for ethnographic fieldwork. Boas had been more than energetic. In 1898 he helped modernize a key journal, the *American Anthropologist*, a task undertaken some years after immigrating from Germany where he had obtained his doctorate in the physical sciences. Trips to Eskimo and Amerindian locations followed, along with coordinating roles in the growth of professional ethnographic and folklore associations. One of Boas's most detailed ethnographies on the Kwakiutl Indians lay buried for decades into the twentieth century until Helen Codere unearthed the seminal work in New York's American Museum of Natural History. Her notes indicate that even the much-respected Boas had been obliged to compromise his fieldwork seriously in the extensive Northwest Territories in the face of desultory private funding for travel and transportation costs (Codere, 1966:xi–xxxii). Expeditionary efforts involving ethnographic fieldwork remained sporadic and often mentor financed until the Carnegie Institution in Washington formed a department of Archeology in 1913. Also significant in the history of financial support for early anthropology was the growing presence of anthropologists on the National Research Council, which had been founded in 1916 in an attempt to further war preparedness (Stocking, 1976a).

The intermittent nature of research patronage in the nineteenth century thus left the developing social sciences without much fiscal sustenance even as public interest grew. There appears little real difference in that context between the smaller donor and the patron of greater means, either with respect to inspiration for benefactions or episodic character of personal largesse. Public enthusiasm over natural wonders and the growth of the metropolis generated both pride and increasing donations to scholarly and urban institutions. Charitable donations expanded to include the immigrants and the urban poor. Nevertheless, the philanthropic impulse, though pervasive, was hardly a valuable corrective to urban poverty or to an increasing desire to place academic science on a secure, sustained footing. Cumulative progress in science clearly required more than the transient, shifting supports offered by even the most generous and discerning of nineteenth-century donors.

Moreover, if the natural sciences and astronomy seem to have fared a bit better in charity history than the social sciences, it now appears less a result of donor disinterest than a desire of philanthropists to attach themselves to what was ameliorative in the sociological imagination. The contemporary theoretical discourses of men such as Franklin H. Giddings and Lester Frank Ward provided broad paradigms of how sociologists thought societies functioned but few insights into the manner in which an enlightened social science could contribute to the alleviation of urban poverty and a concomitant rise in infectious disease. The need of philanthropists to underwrite social welfare activities, and thus to support the applied rather than the pure aspects of science, was, however, hardly unique to the formative social sciences and infused the evolution of physics as well (Kevles, 1987). It seems likely that a greater number of academic institutions and trained scientific scholars were needed in order to clarify the interplay between the theoretical and applied aspects of these fields. The awaiting philanthropic spirit could then be presented with an established attraction whose concerns might more easily conjoin with those of the charitable community.

In particular, the potential donor to scholarly research in the social sciences found few flourishing university systems in which scientific activity actually occurred. The great cosmopolitan universities of our own day were emergent and limited in geographic scope. They were also restricted in Ph.D. production, a fact integral in hindering the growth of stable processes of academic succession upon faculty retirements. Columbia and Chicago, predominant voices in the nation's social science collectivity, struggled along with few students and with only sporadic research funding inappropriate to the urban challenges surrounding them or to the rising Boasian agenda in anthropology (Shils, 1970). Research possibilities in physics were similarly weak, there being no more doctoral productivity near the turn of the century than twenty years before. This relative absence of scholarly growth remained strikingly consistent despite the Cornell ascendancy, the presence of the Ryerson laboratory at Chicago, and Michelson's Nobel (Kevles, 1987:76).

The academic pull of philanthropy near the turn of the century might also have remained underdeveloped because of an additional aspect of apparent university invisibility. As late as 1906, half of America's 600 scientists were clustered in institutions of higher learning on the East Coast. Of these scientists, over 70 percent had received their doctorates abroad. Many youthful scholars therefore had spent much time outside the United States; links to potential donors thus remained less encouraging than if graduate work had been carried out on patriotic home soil (Cattell, 1927). Given the apparent geographic and organizational limitations of the early social scientific enterprise, late nineteenth-century philanthropists understandably clung to their accustomed focus on the natural sciences, natural history museums, and astronomy, while benefactions to charitable agencies in urban centers continued to receive a good measure of philanthropic support. A shift toward uncharted ground involving university endowments and social science support had to await a slightly later time. It was during the first three decades of the twentieth century that those with vast fortunes began to perceive that the science of society could actively inform the character of critical social work interventions and urban social policy development.

Nevertheless, it would be incorrect for a later time and perspective to fault nineteenth-century science patronage for not having helped to underwrite academic specialization and sustained research. First, piecemeal science patronage successfully expanded throughout the nineteenth century despite a lingering heritage of caution toward eleemosynary trusts and organized forms of charitable giving. Second, it seems clear that individual donors more than occassionally provided a greater level of concern and generosity than the parsimonious public purse, whose greatest critic, Simon Newcomb, had accused of a "downright neglect" of American science since the Civil War (Newcomb, 1902).

Third, the accumulation of capital organized into a sustaining endowment was an unusual philanthropic creation in the nineteenth century and without widespread precedent. The Peabody Education Fund, founded in the 1860s, devoted itself largely to the revitalization of educational systems in the devastated South. The Lowell Institute, as generative for science as it proved to be, did not sponsor research and since the 1830s had focused on scientific presentations and lectures for the new professionals but also for the interested public. Even the maintenance of a full activity schedule at the institute was in its earlier years suggestively responsive to fluctuations in the fortunes of the manufacturing mills on whose profits the institute then rested (Weeks, 1966).

A few ingredients seemed necessary in order to place private-sector science funding on a firmer basis than piecemeal individualism had previously allowed. The vast industrially based monetary fortunes of the late nineteenth century were one essential factor, amply played out in foundation growth in the first two decades of the next. Planning and priority setting in science and related support systems was also needed for the evolution of effective endowments and became increasingly so as scientists faced a quickened pace of public enthusiasm and a need to problem solve. In 1905 Henry H. Donaldson, chairman of the Central Branch of the Society of American Naturalists, noted the palpable scientific compulsions of the day and added a veiled reference to a need to dampen contemporary academic competition. "By our Common Methods," he wrote, "we too often seem to advance upon the undiscovered country . . . so that it were done rapidly and before others could arrive" (Donaldson, 1906: 286).

The planning element in the human sciences played a recognized background part in foundation generation as well. As early as 1909, Alida Lattimore had assumed the professional title of social worker and had acknowledged that "indiscriminate charity" aided those who did not warrant it while leaving little fiscal support for the study of "abnormal conditions" in society that provoked charitable needs (Lattimore, 1909:595). An even more august figure had earlier agreed. Edward T. Devine took his doctorate in Germany in economics; he became a "social economist" involved in the Charity Organization Movement and eventually director of the New York School of Philanthropy. In 1906, as president of the National Conference of Charities and Correction, Devine buttressed Lattimore's comments by emphasizing that the dominant mode of "scientific philanthropy" must encompass interventions guided by the causal analysis of poverty and conditions beyond individual control (Devine, 1906:344). Neighboring disciplines of anthropology and sociology were seeking support for empirical work in order to clarify abstract paradigms of society and of cultural evolution. In contrast, social workers such as Lattimore and Devine clearly sought research supports so as to temper arbitrary interventions with understandings of a sociological nature.

A final ingredient in the generation of sustaining endowments for the emergent social sciences was a managerial aspect best articulated for a wide public by Frank Tucker in a 1905 issue of *Charities*, the preeminent journal of scientific philanthropy. Achievement of social betterment, he agreed, was not only tied to charity and environmental understandings but also to the guidance and duties of charity organization trustees and governing boards (Tucker, 1905). According to Tucker, the honorary nature of trusteeship nonetheless demanded a strong professional commitment to grant making and to the production of an annual organizational report, or "activity review," of substantial and critical summary. Further, Tucker's mild admonition to the social stewards of the day to cultivate a "desire to legislate not dominate" carried within it at least two different but related injunctions (Tucker, 1905:295). One injunction entailed the development of textual materials gained from social work practice for the use of the discipline itself. The second seriously urged social work research but only if carried out autonomously from bureaucratic control and disseminated for critical response and application. As Alida Lattimore reiterated four years after Tucker's advice, the reordering of unplanned charity demanded a multicausal approach to class problems and to individual needs, as well as a program of "educating the already educated" (Lattimore, 1909).

The endowed foundations that grew up in the early twentieth century integrated elements of this advice and admonition. Backed by Andrew Carnegie's Gospel of Wealth commentaries, they provided an organizational context for a reworking of the quickened intellectual pulse that to Donaldson had seemed appropriately entrepreneurial yet chaotic. The first major foundations—the Carnegie, Rockefeller, and Russell Sage endowments—followed rapidly on one another between 1902 and 1910 and served as a beneficient catalyst for needy, growing university systems and for academic specialization. Thereafter, foundation work followed public enthusiasms in initial grant-making directions. Although still lacking expeditionary monies for the pervasive Boasian agenda, anthropologists could frequently rely on the Carnegie Institution's support for artifact hunting dedicated to enriching museum collections. Social work profited from the Russell Sage's "social research before social amelioration" stance and from the foundation's perceptive publications in that field (Trattner, 1974). Moreover, if benefactions were increasingly enclosed in permanent philanthropic trusts, scientists managed to retain some of the room for maneuver they had possessed during the previous era of piecemeal patronage. Foundation giving, wrote Raymond Fosdick enthusiastically, was an "adventure."[3] Research results might diverge from anticipated goals; risk taking was therefore inherent in the philanthropic process (Fosdick, 1964). Additionally, foundations tended to adopt a policy of no policy, searching instead to "delicately affiliate" contemporary projects with the uncertainties that lay ahead (Fosdick, 1964:317; Harrar, 1962:vii). Such institutional flexibility might not have been equitably distributed throughout all of the earliest foundations. Nevertheless, the early foundation climate was dominated by a noticeable capacity of research scientists to adapt to foundation priorities and by the potential of trustees to reinterpret broad foundation charters in order to pursue more specialized paths.

If there was little of foundation policy, therefore, foundation programs and projects could nonetheless be developed. If the earliest of foundations favored any programs at all, these were academic in character and drew mainly on social welfare concerns and related social scientific activities (Morison, 1966:78). Admittedly philanthropic support had been long in coming. But so had the empirical study of society and of culture that was increasingly suited to the goals of the modern foundations.

The data of social work were inherently empirical but demanded synthesis and classification. The problem of the early social sciences was the opposite, at least insofar as research requirements were concerned. Nestled at Columbia University, the Boasians aimed at substituting a highly problematic evolutionary paradigm with a detailed view of specific cultures as functioning and integrated societies. Domestic and foreign travel, as well as extensive fieldwork, were a logical and costly accompaniment. Nineteenth-century sociologists had confidently generalized, as Harris rather modestly phrased it, "on the basis of fragmented evidence" (Harris, 1968:254). As a healthy antidote to the initial works of Ward and Giddings stood the mounting studies of urban sociologists at the University of Chicago where the participant-observation techniques of anthropologists were adapted to local community investigations and neighborhood ethnographies.

After nearly two decades of self-financed research, funding finally began to make inroads at the social science departments of Columbia and Chicago universities. The National Research Council recognized anthropology for funding purposes in 1916. In the early 1920s, the sociology department at Chicago received its first external support for research in the form of a $25,000 grant from the Laura Spelman Rockefeller Memorial Foundation. In the light of the long years of sociology without fiscal sustenance, however, it is not surprising that Burgess and Bogue's famous reminiscences of Chicago's earliest years give little space to foundation influence on contemporary endeavors (Burgess and Bogue, 1964). Much pathbreaking work had already been accomplished before the Rockefeller grant; future projects had already been mapped. Only a laconic mention of the Rockefeller subvention appears in the remembrance:

> So they gave us a grant, as I recall of $25,000 for the first year. That wouldn't seem very large for social scientists of the present. But, when you had only $300 for one study, it seemed like a great amount. (Burgess and Bogue, 1964:6)

"The period with funds came suddenly upon us," they added, as it inevitably did to anthropology and social work studies. From the first two decades of the twentieth century onward, American foundations were to help sustain the academic growth and research activities of the social sciences and expanding graduate social work. Organized philanthropy nevertheless continued the familiar nineteenth-century tension between the capacity of donors and their legacies to shift priorities through time and the scientific community's need to change its own interests and to diversify.

NOTES

1. Quoted in Miller (1970:119).
2. See Miller (1970:48) and his prefatory remarks that "there were no general principles governing private philanthropy for scientific purposes . . . idiosyncratic individuals gave a unique flavor to each case" (p. ix).
3. Fosdick was president of the Rockefeller General Education Board, founded in 1902.

2

Kin and Nonkin: The Gradual Life Cycle of Early Foundations

> The father born, the son dying. . . . Yet I do not believe in such things. I leave them for Welshmen and the like.
>
> Margaret George (1986:20)

Andrew Carnegie's injunction that there was a certain "disgrace to dying rich" clearly sounded the background tone of philanthropic giving in the early decades of the twentieth century. At that time in foundation history, however, the immediate task was less one of grant making than of successfully translating broad donor philosophies into tangible arenas of foundation concern. Donor desires to bring about the greatest good for the largest number of Americans were phrased generally enough to encompass a diverse list of projects. They also offered those of a managerial bent a chance to conceptualize a variety of realistic avenues of foundation activity. Always keep the door "a little open to the rare and critical opportunity," wrote James R. Angell of the Carnegie Corporation just ten years after its establishment in 1911 (Angell, 1931:14). Other early participants in foundation life, such as Abraham Flexner, insisted that people with ideas "are best left alone, but if they lack ideas, their situation is not improved when their brains are pooled" (Flexner, 1915a:95).

The first thirty years of the twentieth century was a time of foundation experimentation and priority setting. The direction of grant making was determined by a complex mixture of donor intentions, trustee convictions about the nature of societal needs, and the character of philanthropic management. This chapter outlines trends in the development of major American foundations from their inception to the early 1970s when social gerontology began visibly to penetrate academic life. Only the largest of the early private foundations are surveyed (see Table 2.1); the activities of the corporate and community trusts, the majority of which appeared on the foundation landscape later in time, are presented below during a discussion of gerontology development.

A cardinal problem of the early foundations was not fiscal but organizational in scope. An increase in the number of endowed foundations was spurred by the onset of tax-exempt status in the second decade of the twentieth century. Experimentation in foundation development grew quickly, as did a proliferation of philanthropic institutions endowed by a single donor or his family members. The Rockefeller General Education Board (GEB) was founded in 1902 and was followed only a few years later by the Rockefeller Foundation. The Laura Spelman Rockefeller Memorial Foundation appeared in 1918 and the International Education Board, also a Rockefeller enterprise, in 1923. By the late 1920s, however, there was increasing evidence that the dispersion of philanthropy into related trusts with similar aims meant unnecessary duplication of responsibility (Flexner, 1915a). In 1929, the year of the great Wall Street crash, the four Rockefeller funds were reorganized; the Laura Spelman fund and the International Education Board left the foundation field altogether, and their activities were assimilated into the GEB and the main foundation.

The Carnegie foundation complex was not so numerous and remained rather specialized in function. The Carnegie Institution in Washington was oriented toward the scientific enterprise, the Carnegie Foundation for the Advancement of Teaching fo-

Table 2.1
Selected Early Foundations

NAME	INCORPORATION SITE	INCORPORATION DATE
Carnegie Corporation of New York	New York, NY	1911
The Commonwealth Fund	New York, NY	1918
W.K. Kellogg Foundation	Michigan	1930
Milbank Memorial Fund	New York, NY	1905
New York Foundation	New York, NY	1909
Rockefeller Foundation	New York, NY	1913
Russell Sage Foundation	New York, NY	1907

Note: The Carnegie Institution in Washington (1902) is not listed here because of its self-granting powers. Other Rockefeller funds that later merged into the foundation are discussed in the text.

cused on educational endeavor, and the Carnegie Corporation undertook general-purpose activities. Although overlapping duties were not a pronounced feature of the Carnegie endowments, the existence of overlapping directorates was nonetheless embodied in the competent and experienced figure of Daniel Coit Gilman. His lengthy attachment to higher education, social welfare causes, and the Charity Organization Movement made him a more than suitable candidate for the role of multiple trustee. Gilman was not only a key figure on the boards of the Carnegie Institution and the Carnegie Foundation for the Advancement of Teaching, he also linked Carnegie and Rockefeller trusts through a long-standing membership on the GEB. Other early and significant foundations, such as the Russell Sage and the Milbank Memorial Fund, did not have sister institutions endowed by the same philanthropist and were able to weather the formative age of foundation growth without much overlapping of directorates or organizational modification.

Given Frank Tucker's timely interest in trustee stewardship, it would not be inappropriate to survey a few of the personal characteristics of the early trustees, as well as the relationship of trustee stewardship to foundation grant-making priorities. We lack, of course, the minutiae of board meetings as well as their personality bonds and conflicts. Absent, therefore, is a sense of how the broad donor mandates confronting trustees were invested with actual programming and a unified organizational stamp. However, there remain a few measurable traits that can be utilized to compare the early trustees with their counterparts some sixty years later. We may thus ascertain changes and continuities in person and in profession in order to uncover whether formative experiments in the social organization of philanthropic management have weathered well, poorly, or not at all.

The directing boards of the five great foundations endowed before World War I possessed a number of outstanding features (Table 2.2).[1] Their trustees were of decidedly late age; a few were over eighty years. Businessmen, bankers, attorneys, and university administrators were almost equally represented on the foundation boards, while researchers held a slightly smaller share of the total. Interestingly, at least 25 percent of all of the early trustees served on one or more of the five foundation boards in the sample. Equally as significant was the fact that only 4 percent of the early trustees was related by kinship to original foundation donors. Therefore the separation of endowment organization and managerial control seems a prominent facet of formative foundation life, as was the tendency toward multiple trusteeship.

The elevated age of the first foundation trustees bears comment. Philanthropic trusts were an emergent charitable enterprise. Trustees with managerial expertise had to be drawn from the growing corporate world, from professional associations and societies, and from organizations where fund raising had been a necessary correlate of institutional growth. Many business corporations and nonprofit endeavors began to reach prominence only in the latter half of the nineteenth century. It thus seems likely that only those men and women who were born during or before the Civil War would become suitable candidates for trustee stewardship in the new century.

Prior philanthropic experience also helped to underwrite potential trustee candidacy. On the early Rockefeller Foundation directorate sat Martin Ryerson, a well-known science philanthropist and a trustee at the University of Chicago. Also on the Rockefeller board appeared Starr J. Murphy, counsel to John D. Rockefeller, Dr. Wycliffe Rose, a general agent of the Peabody Education Fund, and Julius Rosenwald, a highly successful merchant, a trustee of Hull House and the Baron de Hirsch fund, and ultimately a donor to his own foundation in 1917. The physician Simon Flexner was initially linked to the new Rockefeller Foundation through his friendship with Daniel Coit Gilman, also an original Rockefeller trustee. The Milbank Memorial Fund boasted Elihu Root, a former secretary of state and a trustee of the Carnegie Institution. The Carnegie foundation complex, however, added a tempering note to the tendency of the larger trusts to depend on trustees derived from the existent philanthropic community. All of the early Carnegie institutions were notable for their ability to attract a series of distinguished university deans and, in the case of Nicholas Murray Butler at Columbia, a university president as well.

Age and philanthropic experience, then, were a necessary but not a sufficient condition of trusteeship. The potential pool of

Table 2.2
Age, Occupational, Relational, and Board Distribution of Trustees of Five Major Foundations at Period of Start-up and 1970

	START-UP PERIOD FIRST DECADE # = 24	1970-71 # = 34
Average Age of Trustee	76 years	59 years
Profession at Appointment		
Executive	25%	44%
Attorney	25%	8%
University Administration	25%	20%
Researcher/Clinical	21%	23%
Other	–	3%
% Trustees Related to Donor	4%	3%

% Trustees on More Than One Board in Sample	25%	8%
% Trustees on Additional Foundation Boards	8%	16%
% Trustees on University Boards	9%	23%
% Trustees Related to Previous Trustees on the Same Board	—	6%
% Trustees Related to Trustees on other Boards in Sample	8%	—

Source: Data derived from foundation annual reports, reviews, and biographical source materials and dictionaries.
Notes: Foundations surveyed were the Commonwealth Fund, the Russell Sage Foundation, the Rockefeller Foundation, the Carnegie Corporation, and the Milbank Memorial Fund. Period of start-up refers to the first decade of each foundation's existence.

trustees from which the stewards were eventually drawn was constrained and occasionally required the addition of university educators who were not unfamiliar with the past century's philanthropic tradition of piecemeal charity. The small number of early foundations also favored interlocking boards of directors. The Carnegie Corporation of New York and the Carnegie Institution in Washington shared the talents of James Merriam, an eminent paleontologist. Simon Flexner, a Rockefeller trustee, served in a similar capacity at the Carnegie Institution. Despite the measured number of trustees who were educators and researchers, philanthropic giving to higher education and to science was soon to become a significant foundation undertaking. The presence of the magnanimous Julius Rosenwald on a critical Rockefeller directorate helped to bring social welfare issues into the funding picture as well.

The trustees of the five major foundations in the 1970s exhibited credentials similar to their counterparts earlier in the century. However, the sixth decade of foundation life saw a preference for trustees who were corporate executives, although the presence of researchers and educators remained pronounced on foundation boards. An increase in corporate executives as foundation trustees may be traced in part to an increased valuation of financial skills in philanthropic management, as well as to a more recent role of executives as foundation donors in their own right.

Sixty years after the major foundations were established, only 3 percent of trustees were related by kinship to the original donors. Philanthropic management continued to maintain a distance from formative endowment organization. Additionally, a definite decline in multiple board memberships within this group of five foundations had occurred. More modern trustees of the original five endowments preferred additional service on the boards of newer foundations or on those of the universities. Indeed the university affiliations of the trustees of the five major boards had increased by 14 percent in sixty years, while the average age of the 1970s trustee was only fifty-nine. It is more than likely that the lower average age of the modern trustee has been encouraged by a need for younger men and women with a recently acquired knowledge base.

Despite differences in age, therefore, there were few real distinctions in the personal characteristics of trustees who served on the major foundation boards at an earlier or later time. There was, however, a striking tendency for multiple board memberships to shift their character over the years from the original foundations to newer, smaller funds or to the boards of American universities. This expansion of trustee ties to the boards of less well-known endowments meant that the influence of the five great foundations had an opportunity to disperse itself over a wide field. It also implied that the development of many American foundations would be characterized by a common set of purposes, as well as the definition of a similar trajectory in general grant-making activities. For example, during the first fifty years of foundation existence, foundation giving was wedded to the growth of American universities. Science and social science research were a significant but more limited attachment (Table 2.3). From 1930 to the 1950s, grants to medical research on the part of seventy-seven large foundations managed to climb a hefty 17 percent; grant making for the social, physical, and biological sciences rose only 6 percent per academic field in the same period. Even in the early 1950s, scientific research remained a minor arena for foundation attention. Only 16 percent of the combined expenditures of seventy-seven larger foundations were then devoted to the scientific enterprise (Table 2.4).

Table 2.3
Affiliations of Individual Research Grants at Seventy-seven Large Foundations, 1953

RECIPIENTS OF GRANTS	% OF TOTAL
Universities	78%
Health Agencies	6%
Research Institutes	6%
Other Affiliates	8%
Unclassified	2%
	100%

Source: Andrews, (1956:275).

Table 2.4
Areas of Foundation Activity, 1968

FIELD	% OF TOTAL
Education	41%
Sciences	14%
International Activities	10%
Health	10%
Welfare	10%
Humanities	3%
Religion	2%
Uncategorized	100%

Source: W. Nielson (1972:Table 3).

The majority of foundation monies went to university development—to building funds, laboratories, and libraries (Andrews, 1956:222–223).

Sometime in the early history of American foundations, a decision had been made and shared among board members: that effective philanthropic work would need to transcend the particular interests of trustees of diverse background, as well as the haphazard nature of nineteenth-century charity and science patronage. Rather than dispense vast sums to a variety of organizations and individuals in an eclectic manner, an intermediary institution was sought that could meet foundation priorities and filter funds to a wider public. This institution was the American university, which was perceived as a preeminent vessel for the seeding and cultivating of the greatest good. It is probable that the numerical strength of university educators helped engender a lasting relationship between organized philanthropy and the university system. But a prominent utilitarian note must have been in the air as well. As early as 1930, the creative president of the Carnegie Corporation, Frederick P. Keppel, had written, "What social instrument is the foundation's nearest relative? I think, without any question, it is the university" (quoted in Morison, 1966:77). This quasi-familial tie has continued well into the latter half of the century.

The kinship aura surrounding foundation and university relations reflected the fact that the "burden" of the major endowments, as Keppel later put it, could be conveniently shifted to other institutional hands. Yet the early link between foundation and universities was not so easily gained or without its persistent detractors. At first it seemed that the Carnegie complex would have the greatest impact on the academy, for it channeled vast sums into college and university systems, which were beset by ill-defined admissions policies and curricula that hardly differentiated them from secondary schools (Morison, 1966:79–80). Plagued by a lack of endowments, inadequate faculty salaries, and a relative absence of scientific instrumentation, the higher education system in the first decades of the century was equally battered by a rising public critique that pointed to the fly-by-night nature of many emergent academic institutions (Morison, 1966:80–81). The Carnegie complex helped define curriculum standards and admissions policies. However, at the same time, it limited its donations to nonsectarian academies and thus provoked a heated response from many of the country's most distinguished and most prestigious universities with long-standing denominational pedigrees. Criticism of the Carnegie reform also grew from the fact that the foundations' influence in structuring university admission requirements quickly developed an impact that stretched far beyond the nonsectarian institutions the Carnegie complex actually endowed. Many in academic life thus concluded that the Carnegie complex had decisively surpassed Frank Tucker's initial desire for a philanthropic management that legislated, not dominated.

The Rockefeller GEB was more diplomatic but equally as influential in standardizing the quality of academic life. By the early 1920s, Rockefeller grants to American institutions of higher learning totaled nearly $60 million (Morison, 1966:85). General university supports, as well as those for specific research projects and scientific activity, began to take on separate existences in the foundation agenda in the late 1920s when venturism in grant making finally addressed itself properly to the GEB's earlier conceptual flexibility. With a turn away from the "advancement of teaching" to the generation of ideas and their applications, a fruitful link could more easily evolve between foundations and university faculty. Indeed the growing presence of researchers on foundation directorates suggested that scientific specialists might soon enjoy a better opportunity of being recognized for funding purposes. The challenge facing the philanthropic trusts was thus not one of judging project worthiness but rather the familiar issue of having insufficient monies for an expanding number of worthy projects.

Grants to universities for specific scientific demonstrations generated another problem in the relationship between foundations and American universities. Both the Carnegie and Rockefeller foundations focused on intensive distributions to projects associated with older academic institutions that were already graced with scientific instrumentation. This foundation activity never assumed the form of a definite policy. For example, foundation annual reports refrain from mentioning any institutional bias or selectivity in grant making. Yet university grant giving for special projects was nevertheless crafted, stated Wycliffe Rose of the GEB, so that already existent peaks in American higher education could be made even higher. Funding thus favored those universities that seemed to be producing the "best science," and did so because these institutions had a tradition of producing the most sophisticated science in the past. Largely excluded from foundation consideration were newer universities that had the potential for growth but had consistently lacked the opportunity to match faculty research talent with sufficient research funding (Sommer, 1987).

Despite these limitations of scope, early American foundations contributed immeasurably to professionalism in higher education as well as to the growth of biomedicine. The behavioral sciences benefited from subventions from the Laura Spelman Rockefeller Memorial Foundation, as did urban sociology. The Spelman fund's innovative aid to Yale's Institute of Human Relations also helped erect an institutional framework for the development of the social sciences and provided for an academic organization where studies in psychiatry, biology, and psychology could coexist with sociocultural endeavors. If interdisciplinary achievements did not yet transcend departmental specialism, other university science grants soon followed and were characterized by a desire for multidisciplinary activity. Among these grants were Rockefeller subventions for psychiatric education in the graduate schools of medicine, Viking Fund attention to physical and cultural anthropology, and the emphasis of the Commonwealth Fund and the Russell Sage Foundation on grant making for medical sociology. The Russell Sage's early commitment to infusing social welfare studies with an environmental agenda led naturally to a significant role for social science in medical and social work interventions.

The influence of the early foundations on academic life was therefore selective but decisive. This influence manifested itself in increasing standardization of curricula and admissions policies and in a rise of scientific endeavor. Overall the social sciences seemed to profit more from foundation interventions than did the natural and physical sciences. Social science enjoyed a closeness to foundation efforts at affecting social reform, or at least was seen as capable of providing data on which enlightened reforms could be based. Social science also blended well with medical and social work interventions and seemed able to adapt comfortably to a foundation focus on issues of public health. Although in retrospect foundation subventions to biomedicine and biomedical research far exceeded those to the emergent social sciences, much pioneering work in social science was funded and included research into small group organization, human sexual behavior, and human relations in industrial contexts. Moreover, early foundations clearly recognized the significance of both the theoretical and applied aspects of sociology and anthropology. In so doing, the formative foundations helped move social science into a developed and visible corner of the academic culture of the day. They thus served to legitimate the social sciences as valid fields of endeavor that possessed both a service function as well as an informed commentary on contemporary existence (Weiss, 1966:183).

Each of the five major foundations had its own pattern of growth, yet foundation interests managed to reach a mutual accommodation nevertheless. Rockefeller gifts were varied and highly responsive to the devastation of World War I with benefactions to the Red Cross and Belgian relief programs. In addition to university endowments, American health and social problems were addressed by the Rockefeller complex in endowments for the International Health Board and in 1917 by support for the School of Public Health at Johns Hopkins under the directorship of William R. Welsh. More specific projects involving the social sciences came under the presidency of Max Mason in the 1920s. The Rockefeller Foundation gifts were small in nature, such as $2,500 to the Royal Anthropological Institute, and were accused of fostering a shotgun approach that favored support for diverse projects while allowing few scholars the sustenance for long-term research. However, social research thrived at the foundation itself, while nearly $3 million was allocated to related research activity at the International Health Board and to the medical education division at Johns Hopkins's new public health facility.

The Milbank Memorial Fund favored public health research as well but soon added a department that dealt with social welfare supports and a range of urban and rural health demonstration programs. The fund interested itself in the diseases of infancy, mental disorders, and the dynamics of metropolitan and tenement life. Only seventeen years after its founding in 1905, the Milbank endowment sponsored a conference involving leaders in social science research. Scientists were brought together in order to exchange ideas on a research agenda for social studies in health, hygiene, and adult life. Such research, however, was overshadowed by issues of public health and infectious disease. Biomedical research at that time was hardly integrated into emergent work in medical sociology.

Under Dr. James Rowland Angell, the Carnegie Corporation had launched its campaign to standardize university campuses. Frederick P. Keppel's long and distinguished reign at the Carnegie began in 1923 and ushered in a new and innovative focus on the fine arts and adult education. Carnegie gifts to settlement houses continued, and an interest in the social sciences was reflected in Carnegie funding for the National Research Council and the Bureau of Economic Research, both of which had their own grant-making powers. However, these agencies could not really compensate for the fact that ten years after Carnegie's founding, only 3.7 percent of its monies went to nonmedical research. Eleven percent of the Carnegie grants was channeled into graduate medical education, and at least 85 percent of the Carnegie grant making was devoted to general-purpose sums for college and university systems. Between 1910 and 1925, the Russell Sage Foundation clearly evinced its lasting interest in social welfare. Even in its earliest years, the Russell Sage produced benchmark volumes in social welfare studies, including the books *Social Work* and *Social Work Administration* edited by Margaret B. Hodges. During the same fifteen years the Commonwealth Fund focused on psychiatric social work as well as on the status of graduate medical education. The W. K. Kellogg Foundation, another early fund, similarly aimed at grant making for medical education, while the smaller New York Foundation gave short-term grants to settlement houses, medical charities, and psychiatric medicine at New York's Bellevue Hospital. Despite some pronounced similarities in grant-making directions, the earliest foundations differed significantly in the extent to which grants were term grants, and thus limited in time, or took the form of endowments whose dividends could be drawn upon over a lengthy period. Eventually a few of the Rockefeller endowments were allowed to be committed to purposes other than those originally intended. However, grant making was largely of the short-term variety and remains so today. Although foundation grants may therefore prove innovative, the predominance of term grants tends to lend a note of program or project insecurity to any emergent enterprise.

Just how the foundation propensity for the term grant has affected the social scientific community is subject to conflicting interpretation. On the one hand, term grants induce a research situation characterized by a search for quick applications or outcomes. Additional inquiries that could clarify the results of the original research must then become a subject of time-consuming grant proposal writing. More than one scientist has appropriately complained that it now takes more time to write foundation and federal grant proposals than it does to do the suggested research (Sommer, 1987).

Endowed research funds, on the other hand, further stability in project investigations. Nevertheless, close collegial relationships may arise during lengthy research projects and promote a lesser degree of scientific entrepreneurship. Whether to pool the academic brains over time or to leave room for Dr. Angell's "rare" and individually crafted insight is not, however, a major question on the contemporary foundation agenda. Endowment worth has risen over the years. Large amounts can be given to universities over the short term, while the door can be left open for smaller awards to individuals whose research may represent a pioneering direction.

The early 1970s witnessed some changes of emphasis in foundation giving but few real structural shifts. An interest in population problems grew, as did associated social science research. But medical education remained the great attraction. For example, at the Rockefeller Foundation, the $500,000 allocated to social science in 1970 was literally dwarfed by $44 million worth of expenditures on biomedical, demographic, and related concerns. At the Carnegie Corporation, social science research monies were still limited but creatively diversified in their support of topics ranging from health policy interventions to alternative approaches to child rearing. The Commonwealth Fund continued its traditional interest in medical education and community health issues.

From about 1935 onward, a period in which short-term grants came to be favored, a restricted but distinctive trend in grant making arose. This trend did not diverge from a donor desire to promote social betterment; rather, it supplemented this focus with direct grants to university scientists for the study of disadvantaged populations and social minorities. As early as 1935, an interest in race and racism appeared in the Rockefeller agenda along with psychiatric concerns. At the Milbank Memorial Fund, aging studies and notice of America's growing elderly population had already made a measured entry into foundation deliberations. Though seemingly overwhelmed by ongoing attention to the arts, libraries, and universities, minority issues also began to receive a limited attention at the Carnegie Corporation.

By the 1960s, foundations began to demonstrate a quicker tempo of grant making to studies of older people and minorities. With joint support from the Ford Foundation, the Russell Sage

Foundation produced Matilda White Riley's Aging and Society series in 1964; shortly after, it sponsored a meeting on the aging process and its link to social policy. The New York Foundation continued its interest in the support of settlement houses and sponsored research grants to a small number of social scientists. Under the leadership of Alan Pifer in the 1960s, however, the more substantially endowed Carnegie Corporation entered in a decisive way into the support of American social minorities. Foundations had spent more than five decades in a highly purposeful attempt to build, expand, and improve the country's university systems. Having succeeded in their attempt, it now seemed incumbent upon them to ensure that all Americans, of all backgrounds and economic status, would be able to enjoy the full fruits of foundation activities.

This foundation endeavor encompassed more than university grant making. Through time, there were continuities in support for medical research, public health demonstrations, and social service agencies. A specific focus on racial, ethnic, and age categories in society began early in foundation development and continued into the 1970s. Grant making to the social sciences remained constrained nonetheless, and there appeared little effort to mesh what few later-life studies foundations had sponsored with reforms in the graduate medical curriculum or with biomedical interventions. Social medicine and medical sociology owe some of their origins to early foundation efforts, but these efforts were not a prominent aspect of the general foundation community and quickly lost ground to preemptive university commitments.

Although it has been impossible to catalog all of the early foundation accomplishments, it still seems evident that the social context of foundation work was as important in determining grant-making directions as the nature of trustee stewardship or organization. The strength of urban poverty and disease invoked a logical foundation response in the form of medical research and social welfare supports. However, the foundation attachment to university systems requires an explanation beyond that of mere context. It points to the influence of university educators and researchers on critical foundation directorates. The use of universities as repositories of foundation responsibilities could not have arisen without a growing collectivity of academically inclined trustees to whom the acquisition of knowledge was a necessary accompaniment to enlightened social reform.

Given continuing foundation attention the alleviation of urban poverty and to standardizing academic life, the study of older adults and the aging process was not one of those specific topics that received serious foundation consideration. This was true even though it was clear by the 1970s that changes in the American demography and in the social sciences had brought a range of problems surrounding later life into the public eye, as well as into an established place within federal granting agencies. Over the years, the thrust of foundation activity had remained selectively responsive to overwhelming conditions of poverty in metropolitan centers and to the chaotic character of the early institutions of higher learning. A clear response to anticipated or potential social problems was never a foundation specialty or a key concern.

NOTE

1. Data for this discussion are derived directly from the annual reports and related presidential messages of the following foundations: Rockefeller, Milbank Memorial Fund, Carnegie Corporation, Russell Sage Foundation, New York Foundation, and the Commonwealth Fund. Annual reports surveyed consisted of those associated with the first years of the foundations through 1975.

3

Charity, Sociology, Ethnography

> Teachers of Sociology will find their most appreciative audiences, their most promising and ambitious pupils not in the classroom or the college . . . but in the charity conference, if they will condescend to seek them there.
>
> Frederick Howard Wines (1898:51)

American universities slowly welcomed the advent of professional anthropology, sociology, and social work. Their entrance onto the academic scene occurred during a twenty-year transition period that separated piecemeal patronage to science in higher education and the real beginnings of foundation support for academic research. If the statistician Frederick Wines could refer to the condescending attitudes of sociologists toward the friendly visitors, it was only because the scientific nature of sociology had become increasingly acknowledged. Nevertheless, a desire to use sociological knowledge and methods in order to spur social reform united academician and untutored charity worker alike. Indeed, the well-known Columbia University anthropologist, Elsie Clews Parsons, had energetically wed "dynamic" sociology, "scientific philanthropy," and ethnography shortly before the nineteenth century drew to a close. This chapter surveys the influence of foundation philanthropy on the academic growth of the social sciences and social work. Also discussed is the role of American foundations in fostering independent lines of research and departmental specialization within these disciplines.

Urban sociology at the University of Chicago had diversified roots. To some extent, the origins of early sociology at Chicago can be traced to the growing contributions of early social work. In the late nineteenth century, extensive surveys of tenement life conducted at Hull House in Chicago and in lower-income neighborhoods in New York provided a series of precedents on which sociology's study of metropolitan indigence and immigration could later be built. In 1908 Sophonisba Brekenridge and Edith Abbott of the Chicago School of Civics and Philanthropy began a pathbreaking inquiry into the integration of southern European immigrants into Hull House activities. They also compiled a growing amount of data on the customs and culture of immigrants in specific ethnic neighborhoods (Burgess and Bogue, 1964:4). Despite such research, the concept of charity work as an art was still very much evident in the second decade of the twentieth century (Crothers, 1911). Nevertheless, the contemporary mood had clearly begun to favor infusing friendly visiting with sophisticated organizing principles. Chicago sociologist Charles Henderson hoped the consistent use of these principles would overcome what he called the mere "meddling" of the charity workers and derive directly from Dr. Mathew Arnold's notion that "whatever it is our duty to act, those matters also it is our duty to study" (quoted in Henderson, 1900:253).

Urban sociology also grew from a need to examine human behavior in a metropolitan environment. Field studies were necessary if the ties between behavior and environmental influences were to be uncovered. Graduate students at Chicago worked with grid maps of the city and with extensive interview schedules in order to plumb the social organization of diverse ethnic groups in metropolitan wards and localities.[1] A more developed focus on the socioeconomic forces underlying urban life began in 1916, a few years before the sociology department received its first grant from the Laura Spelman Rockefeller fund. Although the Chicago urbanists contributed detailed distributional maps of almost every facet of metropolitan life—including the location of all of Chicago's movie theaters and restaurants—they are thus best linked to contemporary social science through their emphasis on ethnic group relations. Equally contributory to the science of society was their demonstration that the city, despite its diversity, was an integrated settlement as well as a place whose lifeways were clearly distinct from those of rural villages and towns. We have seen that Chicago sociologist W. I. Thomas had been highly unsuccessful in attracting science patronage to the sociology department at the turn of the century. Nearly twenty years later, however, he was singularly competent at mounting a series of self-financed trips to Eastern Europe. Thomas's studies of Polish peasants on home turf and in Chicago's neighborhoods ultimately did much to reaffirm the sociology department's commitments to ethnic studies, as well as to the ethnographic and comparative methodologies of the related discipline of anthropology (Shils, 1970).

Scientific philanthropy was also making inroads into academic life. In 1920 the Chicago School of Civics and Philanthropy became part of the University of Chicago. A parallel movement of charity work education into the university system occurred in New York City when the New York School of Philanthropy emerged as the basis for the foundation of a graduate social work faculty at Columbia University. Yet in the early decades of the twentieth century, many critics hesitated to term social work a true profession. Abraham Flexner, who frequently offered incisive commentaries on early foundation activities, now spoke out just as incisively about the unpaid nature of charitable work with the poor, the homeless, and the aged (Flexner, 1915b). Moreover, there appeared little actual relationship between the social work treatment of individuals and clarified treatment goals. Finally, Flexner insisted that environmental causes needed to be built into an analysis of individual pathologies. To a certain extent, the desire for a more evolved sociological contribution to social work practice began to be fulfilled in 1917 with the publication of Mary

Richmond's important work, *Social Diagnosis*. Richmond's volume, however, also underscored the tendency for emergent social work to be a consumer of the research conclusions and concepts of other fields rather than a research producer in its own right. The research activities of the charity workers at Hull House and in New York had not dampened this trend. Its history was lengthy and was rooted in the nature of interpersonal ties among the nineteenth-century community of scholars and in the character of late-nineteenth-century academic publications.

Daniel Coit Gilman, first president of Johns Hopkins and a Rockefeller trustee, had been particularly impressed with the work of the Charity Organization Movement in England. Together with journalist and social worker John Finley, Gilman was instrumental in opening a Baltimore chapter in 1881. A series of critical evaluations of the charity organization's work, however, led both Gilman and Finley to the conclusion that sociological studies of the causes of poverty needed to be integrated into the activities of the charity workers in order to improve their skill and effectiveness (Gettleman, 1979:65). Social practice, admitted Henderson at Chicago, seemed to require "scientific demands," while in 1891 a leading charity periodical, *Charities Review*, billed itself accommodatingly as a journal of "practical sociology." Henderson was not only a sociology professor at Chicago University in the 1890s. He was also an editor of the *American Journal of Sociology*, as well as the president of the Twenty-eighth National Conference on Charities. By the end of the nineteenth century, Louisa Lee Schuyler, director of the New York State Charities Association, confidently stated that the New York charity societies seemed less philanthropic in design than sociological in nature (Gettleman, 1979:68).

In order to utilize sociology for its own objectives, it was incumbent upon the growing field of social work to provide an institutional context for the transmission of knowledge and for the process of socializing students to a professional role. In this respect, the fact that a large number of charity workers were geographically dispersed over broad stretches of the country proved an impediment. With the exception of the new schools at Chicago and Columbia, there was a relative absence of academic institutions within which an agenda for professional social work could be systematized or where scholarly self-scrutiny could take place.

The growth of scientific philanthropy in the nineteenth century had received its greatest impetus from charitable need among the urban poor. Another spur to growth derived from the dearth of public mechanisms of relief. Private benevolent agencies abounded in major American cities. Smaller charitable aid associations linked to the Charity Organization Movement grew quickly in metropolitan centers as immigration from Eastern Europe increased. In 1878, Philadelphia was home to 800 of such groups. During the time Charles Henderson was writing about practical sociology at Chicago, the Charity Organization Movement encompassed twenty-five cities. The long-term effectiveness of this organization was nevertheless hindered by its tendency to view charity as a form of spiritual or moral uplift rather than a direct response to a need for material and social supports (Trattner, 1974:84). The spiritual and moral demeanor of charity began to give way to scientific demonstrations only as student social workers consistently participated in an academic context where a knowledge of social science was considered a critical adjunct of the social work curriculum (Lubove, 1974).

Similar to the development of sociology, the beginnings of anthropology were characterized by a few struggling academic departments and a lack of funding sources for research. What has been termed the early "period without funds" in sociology coincided with the period of "object orientation" in anthropological studies (Stocking, 1976a). Natural history museums and anthropological museum collections had profited immeasurably from nineteenth-century piecemeal patronage. For purposes of public display, Amerindian artifacts were cataloged and grouped according to distinguishing traits and styles. The resultant culture areas were believed to be vaguely representative of human populations. The equation of a group of artifactual traits with actual patterns of human organization did not long stand up to ethnographic inquiry or to the coming tests of ethnoarcheological scrutiny (Gould, Koster, and Sontz, 1969). Nevertheless, public interest in anthropology was high, and professional anthropological societies grew steadily between 1900 and 1920. The production of researchers with doctorates in anthropology was, however, limited and largely confined to Columbia, Chicago, and Berkeley. Anthropology continued to be taught at nearly forty smaller colleges by those who called themselves sociologists (Stocking, 1976a:9).

With the establishment of the National Research Council by the Carnegie complex in 1916, fieldwork expeditions became increasingly likely. Ethnographic studies of human interaction supplemented culture area presentations in the museums. This "integrationalist approach" in anthropology signaled the onset of the study of culture and social organization by a resident fieldworker. It also signaled a need to study the environment that traditional societies inhabited. In outlook and in method, the "integrationalist approach" was thus similar to urban sociology at Chicago. In just another few decades, the work of anthropologist Robert Redfield would clearly echo W. I. Thomas's studies of Polish peasants. Historian George Stocking has written that the personal networks of the early anthropologists were constrained. There were few academic departments, and Fellows of the American Anthropological Association numbered only 300. It could equally be argued, however, that this "intellectual endogamy" may have been more apparent than real (Stocking, 1976a:8). The early anthropologists had much in common with their counterparts in urban sociology at Chicago. This intellectual tie was underscored by the marriage of the daughter of Dr. Robert Park, a Chicago urbanist, to Robert Redfield shortly after the anthropologist had completed a course in sociology at that university.

Dr. Elsie Clews Parsons was a transitional figure. Parsons took her undergraduate degree from Barnard College in 1896 and progressed to a master's degree in history only a year later. A doctoral degree in that field followed in 1899 for which Parsons wrote a dissertation on the nature of colonial legislation on education. Parsons's doctoral dissertation became the first of her many works to be published and was soon followed by *The Family* in 1905.

Parsons seems to have pursued a career quite separate from that of her husband, an attorney and New York City congressman from 1905 to 1911. She also deftly skirted the growing personal and intellectual rivalry between anthropologist Frank Boas and Franklin H. Giddings, a sociologist who had served as her dissertation mentor. Eventually Parsons turned enthusiastically to the study of anthropology and exhibited a developing interest in native Americans, folklore, and the manner in which social forces influenced individual behavior. Independently wealthy, Parsons funded many Columbia graduate students' fieldwork. Personal patronage went to the American Folklore Society as well, while her growing professional status within anthropology was enhanced by a presidency of the American Ethnological Society.

Parsons's extensive fieldwork with the Tewa and Pueblo Indians, as well as her rich associational life and charitable spirit, have been sufficient to place her among the founders of American anthropology. In contrast, her teaching methods have been largely ignored, though her turn-of-the-century journal article, "Fieldwork in Teaching Sociology," was prominent enough in its day (Parsons, 1900). In her seminal article, Parsons had emphasized that many of the "pathological" conditions the charity movement hoped to ameliorate were also a valid object of sociological analysis. During a course in "descriptive sociology" at Barnard College, she challenged her students to visit families associated with the Charity Organization Society, as well as to engage in extensive interviews with other household members and neighbors. These interviews were similar to those carried out in Chicago by graduate students in sociology and entailed inquiries about work, voting, shopping, neighboring, and other social patterns. Parsons was highly interested in human relationships. She was delighted to find that an evaluation of the student interview schedules clearly showed that family ties tended to stretch far beyond the household. Domicile and kinship, she concluded, were discrete concepts. More than that, she argued, these differences should become part of the charity worker's tool kit for effecting enlightened service delivery and social reform.

The Barnard students were not only scientific in intent. During their short fieldwork trips, they also carried with them a spirit of moral uplift normally associated with the friendly visitors. Parsons advised them to urge thrift and cleanliness on the indigent families and, where possible, to be instrumental in finding those interviewed appropriate employment. What seems different about Parsons's work and that of the friendly visitors was her use of specific methods of data collection, as well as a type of data presentation and interpretation that permitted research results to be generalized to a broader sample of urban families.

Parsons's studies of the urban poor lacked the participant method of Nels Anderson and W. I. Thomas at Chicago. These methods would have required the on-site residence of Parsons and her students with the sample families and was not a viable teaching technique given the youthful age and elevated social status of the women registered for her course. But Parsons soon began to adopt these community study methodologies in her career as an anthropologist. Though she turned increasingly toward ethnology and folklore, it was clear that she had left behind a significant corpus of work that integrated some of the best features of scientific philanthropy and the emergent social sciences. In the years after her short stay at Barnard College, social work, sociology, and anthropology appear to have begun their academic divergence. Since federal support for academic endeavors was slight and neglectful, much of this divergence was dependent on patrons such as Parsons and the early foundation community.

Personal philanthropy continued to embrace social science and social work during the era of Parsons's research at Barnard. Morris K. Jessup, a banker and a businessman, sat on the board of the American Museum of Natural History and had served as a trustee of the Peabody Education Fund. Jessup died in 1908 and thus did not participate in the formative activities of the major foundations. This seems unfortunate since his varied foundation work in the nineteenth century and his position as the treasurer of the smaller John F. Slack Fund might have rendered him an appropriate candidate for trustee stewardship on one of the later, more well-endowed philanthropic trusts. Jessup's own benefactions ranged from periodic gifts to Columbia's Union Theological Seminary to $100,000 to the American Museum of Natural History for the purpose of erecting statuaries of scientists. Although Jessup's gifts were not targeted toward increasing museum collections, his generosity spurred further donations to the famous natural history museum and helped to provide an institutional framework within which object-oriented anthropology could grow and be critically evaluated (Gilman, 1907). Jacob Henry Schiff served as a trustee of the New York Foundation and of the Baron de Hirsch Fund. An extraordinarily significant financier, Schiff was to donate heavily to New York's Montefiore Hospital, the Henry Street Settlement, and a student hall for Barnard College. The Barnard subvention brought him decisively in the growing philanthropic direction of the Carnegie and Rockefeller trustees, who were becoming increasingly attached to academic and university funding supports. At the same time, Schiff's more modest donations went to Jessup's favorite philanthropic haunt, the natural history museum in New York.

Foundation activity began to influence the growth of anthropology after 1916 when anthropologists gained a growing voice on the National Research Council. The Carnegie Institution had established a department of prehistoric archeology in 1913, which successfully supported archeological surveys of the United States and contributed to expanding museum collections. Anthropologists also joined the Social Science Research Council (SSRC) in 1925. The SSRC received considerable backing from the Rockefeller and Carnegie foundation complexes and engendered a small but steady growth in supports for fieldwork activity.

In the 1930s, New Deal politics brought a federal interest to social welfare concerns. Foundations also moved toward support for social welfare interventions if these were informed by social scientific concepts and by sociological understandings of lower-income neighborhoods. However, contributions to social service agencies were heavily outweighed by those to university systems that were increasingly seen as a major vehicle for dispensing essential foundation commitments (Stocking, 1976a:11). As foundation support for the growth and expansion of academic departments rose, the museum orientation in anthropology declined, and fieldwork assumed a critical role in the discipline. By 1940, America could boast twenty academic departments of anthropology. Columbia, Chicago, and Berkeley remained prominent, but the opportunity to teach anthropology and to do research in the field was becoming more equitably dispersed throughout the country.

A glance at some of the published anthropological work of the 1930s indicates that funding resources for fieldwork were limited but singularly effective in moving anthropologists out of the academic armchair.[2] Fred Eggan's classic studies of Amerindian kinship organization and acculturation were funded by grants from major foundations dispersed to the department of anthropology at the University of Chicago. Julian Steward's theories concerning social organization as an adaptive feature of a specific environment evolved during fieldwork trips to Amerindians of the Great Basin and were funded by joint grants from the University of California and the SSRC (Stocking, 1976b:234, 369).

Sociology's period without funds had ended in the 1920s. The Laura Spelman Rockefeller fund was the first benefactor of urban sociology at Chicago, but its reach extended slowly to other departments as well. In 1923, it helped establish the National Social Science Research Council (NSSRC), an organization that accounted for the increased support to a growing number of universities. NSSRC funding lasted over a decade at Chicago and provoked investigations into ethnic groups and neighborhoods, urban gangs, urban cultural life, and urban topography (Burgess and Bogue, 1964:6-7). There is no doubt that federal Works Progress Administration (WPA) funding of sociology momentarily overwhelmed the foundation role in supporting scholarly activities, but foundation monies continued to pour into the university systems and helped promote the observation at Chicago that "there were as many viable research projects as there were graduate students to pursue them" (Burgess and Bogue, 1964:8). A permanent research endowment at Chicago was organized in 1946 with the aid of the Wieboldt Foundation. This grant affirmed Chicago's urban sociology as preeminent in the field, even as newer sociology departments opened at Harvard, Yale, Northwestern, Michigan, and Wisconsin. Graduate students from Chicago continued to assume academic positions at these and other developing sociology departments until the early 1950s. At that time, Columbia University's sociology department began to turn away from community studies and urban surveys to focus instead on sociological theory and hypothesis testing. The emergence of academic social work entailed not only a necessary growth of university departments; it also required an advanced education for casework skills. Increasingly these skills involved psychotherapeutic interventions whose usage was aided by a growing public and professional acceptance of Freudian psychology (Lubove, 1974:194; Trattner, 1974). As psychiatric social work developed, the professional status of social workers grew. Social work research seemed a secondary preoccupation and largely derivative of social science. The role of the major foundations in the evolution of social work was a multifaceted one yet realistically oriented toward supporting the refinement of casework theory and methods. Rockefeller subventions for psychiatric medicine undoubtedly helped integrate psychology into social work education. Moreover, the Russell Sage Foundation had earlier published studies of life, labor, and education among indigent urban populations. These publications manifested the foundation interest in supporting the development of educational and textual materials in the field of social work. They also emphasized, however, that social work was a field designed to diagnose and to treat individuals; social research, in contrast, should provide the type of social and cultural knowledge that could enrich casework skills and enlighten treatment outcomes. Some of the first structural changes in the new curriculum at the Graduate School of Social Work at Columbia University entailed the inclusion of course work in sociology. The Russell Sage Foundation took much of the lead in curriculum planning by funding a continuing series of background studies of urban living conditions. In 1929 the Russell Sage Foundation began publication of the *Social Work Year Books* (still published as the *Encyclopedia of Social Work*).

The transformation of scientific philanthropy into a full-fledged social work profession was immeasurably aided by foundation support for settlement agencies. The growth of the settlement agencies also meant the growth of administrative positions into which trained social workers could move. Additionally a new field for clinical placements was opened. Administrative work nevertheless removed the social worker from research opportunities. The development of agency slots for student placements also enhanced the tendency for casework to continue its position of dominance in the field (Larson, 1977). Foundation activity actually did little to aid the development of a social work research component. Intent on fostering advanced graduate training and the development of an increased number of social work departments in the universities, the Rockefeller Foundation donated healthy sums to emergent social work faculties and to efforts at standardizing graduate curricula. Even after World War II, social work maintained its position as a user of other specialists' research. By mid-century, however, the National Association of Social Workers instituted its first research section; the 1970s witnessed the appearance of two new scientific journals: *Social Work Research* and the *Journal of Social Services Research* (Polansky, 1975).

In 1950 the National Science Foundation (NSF) opened its doors in Washington. Although entitled a "foundation," the NSF was actually a publicly supported entity, and its appearance signaled the onset of what one prominent sociologist, Robert Merton, termed "the public business of science." Until the 1950s, however, it was the private American foundations that figured most substantially in university development, the growth of social research, and the advancement of professional social work.

It needs to be remembered that the major foundations were established at a time when the social sciences were still strongly tied to abstract theories of society and social evolution based primarily on anecdotal evidence supplied by travelers and missionaries. Scholars often ranked societies on a rather mythical evolutionary scale that expectedly located the traditional or "primitive" cultures at the bottom and the "advanced" or Western civilizations at the top. More scholarly attention was given to classifying cultures than to uncovering the interrelatedness of social and political organizations or to elucidating the link between kinship structure and the environment.

Those nineteenth-century social scientists who concerned themselves almost exclusively with Western civilizations showed an equal predilection for imaginative analysis without, however, grounding opinions in empirical work. Shortly after the General Education Board was founded in 1902, Lester Frank Ward proved himself a master at using mental logic alone to reach untested conclusions about the nature and functioning of society. While reviewing a contemporary book on social evolution, he noted approvingly that the volume was highly theoretical. "This is not a criticism of the book," stated Ward; in fact, "it is one of the beauties of it" (quoted in Harris, 1968:254).

Early foundation work can be criticized for the fact that the ethnographies it sponsored led eventually to a focus on how the parts of a society were related in an integrated yet static fashion. The realities of social conflict and cultural adaptation within a changing environment were largely overlooked for many decades. Foundation support for the integrationalist approach in anthropology also deemphasized problems of social conflict and individual competitiveness by helping researchers better to link the culture areas of the museums with meaningful units of kinship and social organization (Eggan, 1968:126–128). Nevertheless, foundation subventions to research in sociology and anthropology guided the early social scientists toward the empirical study of society and away from the illusory concepts of "evolutionary reconstruction" (Harris, 1968:254). This was indeed a prominent contribution of foundation gifts and provided the social work profession with refined observations and systematized data that could improve clinical interventions.

Foundation support for academic social work, sociology, and anthropology occurred in a grant-making environment as yet unpenetrated by federal bureaucracies. Even the previously active Bureau of Ethnology, originally directed by J. W. Powell, ceased to keep up its initial momentum after the death of its director two years into the twentieth century. In an age when there were few precedents for massive grant making, the major foundations carried out a broad mandate to do the "greatest good for the greatest number" through sizable grants to American universities and the direct sponsorship of specific research projects. In the process, foundations exerted an important influence on the academic specialization of sociology and anthropology, as well as on the academic restructuring of social work education. If early anthropology and sociology shared methodologies and a penchant for functionalist analysis, foundation grant giving ensured that anthropological fieldworkers were increasingly free to examine ideas and concepts gained at home in the light of experiences derived from research in other parts of the world. With foundation support, social work began to specialize and to define its casework focus as well. During the early twentieth century, it began to diverge from anthropology and sociology and established its own academic departments and graduate curricula with aid from the philanthropic trusts. By the early 1930s, the chaotic and fly-by-night character of American universities had begun to pass; the slow yet confident separation of social research from social practice had also begun to strengthen itself within the university system. This academic partition ultimately left lingering difficulties for future scholars in interdisciplinary fields to overcome. But after many decades of foundation activity, this partition seemed a welcome one. It represented what Raymond B. Fosdick, president of the Rockefeller Foundation, might have called "the first faint signs of harvest" (Fosdick, 1964:17).

NOTES

1. See Burgess and Bogue (1964:3).
2. See the articles in Stocking (1976b).

4

The Unreclaimed Land: Social Gerontology as Area Study

> On the small farms then, the old do not retire.
> Conrad M. Arensberg and Solon T. Kimball (1968:159)
>
> Tell me what science can do for Grandma.
> President Lyndon Johnson[1]

The past two chapters have discussed foundation responses to a need for social reform in the early twentieth century. The way in which foundation trustees tended to fulfill their mandate through the use of educational mechanisms has been highlighted. This is not to state that foundations were innovative in provoking university growth and academic specialization. Rather, they are best seen as catalysts that inspired those already inspired with funds for social research that was empirical in nature. In the case of social work, foundations propelled an existent movement toward educational reform and professionalism.

Even with hindsight, however, it would be misleading to compare the growth of social work as an academic discipline with the process of "enclosure" into university systems that McCaughey has argued was commonplace in early twentieth-century academic life (McCaughey, 1984). In the late nineteenth century, charitable endeavors were undertaken by a broad voluntary community. Increasingly the legitimacy for undertaking charity work moved from the voluntary community into the private universities, which demanded course work, training, and clinical placements. Having identified such an academic enclosure, it is nevertheless necessary to understand any remaining link between voluntary charitable activity and professional social work. Not to do so is to regard academic specialization as an end point and not as a process of development that may continue to require foundation support at some future time.

The advent of the trained social work professional tended to endow charity workers with a lower status than they had enjoyed in the heyday of the Charity Organization Movement (Lubove, 1974). The distinction between volunteer and professional, however, did not imply an end to personal interactions among those who were paid and those who went unpaid for their services. What this distinction ultimately brought about was a redefinition of responsibilities and the emergence of professional social workers as supervisors of critical volunteer activities. It is largely this supervisory role of the social worker that continues to link professional organization with public activity. The relationship between professional and volunteer caregiver is especially crucial in our own age when volunteerism has become an integral part of service delivery to a variety of elderly and lower-income populations.

A later chapter discusses the issue of creative volunteerism among older adults. These older adults are in their "third age" and will continue to seek re-entry into the labor force in paid or voluntary capacities. A growing amount of older adult activity in the labor force invites us to redefine the character of supervisory roles once again. It also challenges foundations to redirect priorities in research supports and in program maintenance (Nee and Bracco, 1986) as well as to renew subventions to what might seem already crystallized academic fields.

In the following two chapters I survey the growth of late-age studies as a subfield of anthropology, sociology, and social work.

SOCIAL GERONTOLOGY AS AREA STUDY 51

The growth of gerontological studies has proceeded from a small and cautious base that was established during the early decades of foundation development. Patterns in the production of doctoral degrees provide a quantitative assessment of subfield development. A discussion of dissertation topics is also offered in order to understand whether independent lines of research have been supplemented by interdisciplinary interests. An overview of gerontology instruction in American institutions of higher learning is presented in the light of manpower and training needs and in view of research demands.

A continuing problem in the history of science is the tendency for contemporary scholars to draw a direct line of connection between a pioneering idea in the distant past and a topical discovery of note. Though the ancient quest to retain the properties and energies of youth is a still-living concern, systematic studies of aging are relatively new on the intellectual scene and less prone to what Robert Young called a "convenient search for anticipation."[2] For example, the separation of the aged from other indigent groups for purposes of charitable support was clearly not a preoccupation of the early foundations. This inattention, however, did not necessarily mean a lack of concern. A variety of historical factors acted to limit foundation grant making to the elderly. It should be remembered that foundation trustees reacted largely to problems of scale in society—including issues of public health, education reform, pauperism, and relief. In the main, poverty seemed embedded in processes of immigration and industrialization in what are today termed primary and secondary cities. W. Andrew Achenbaum's survey (1978:86) of the changing social valuation of the American aged in the nineteenth and twentieth centuries underscores that the strength of old-age dependency at the time of early foundation growth was not at all apparent. Many viewed older adults as an insignificant link in the chain that joined industrialization, poverty, and unemployment. Problems of the aged were seen as related to the aging process; they were also enhanced by "fixed" conditions of later life, such as expected physical or mental declines. Since the elderly, in addition, were believed to be minor consumers of philanthropy or of charitable aid (Achenbaum, 1978:85), foundations turned logically toward a more visible and youthful population sector for initial granting considerations.

A relative absence of visibility on the charitable scene was a real and vital phenomenon. Older adults were still enmeshed in the extended family and subject to intrafamilial supports of a diverse nature. Elsie Clews Parsons had uncovered some of these supports during her teaching career and fieldwork exercises at Barnard College. Although the elderly often lived in residences beyond the observable household, they remained tied to younger family members through food, clothing, and other exchanges. Given the "fixed" problems of later life and the relative absence of data that suggested an increase in old-age dependency, more youthful populations quickly became the appropriate object of foundation attention and interest.

Existent legislation must have reinforced this process. Although limited later-life pensions were available in some states, much contemporary legislative activity was geared toward the enforcement of aid obligations to aged relatives on the part of younger family members. Attempts to widen state aid proved unfruitful for alleged lack of need and because of contemporary conceptions of close familial networks. These were viewed not only as tenaciously held together but were also regarded in a moralistic light. In Massachusetts, conditions of the elderly in the first ten years of the twentieth century were deemed tolerable; moreover, "pensions would be expensive, destroy thriftiness, disintegrate the family, and lower wages, and . . . they might also be unconstitutional" (Achenbaum, 1978:83).

For our purposes, the issue of constitutionality is less important than reigning notions of thriftiness and the belief that state aid would decouple family relationships. The emphasis on thrift makes the contemporary legislative activity seem close in spirit to that of the Charity Organization Movement. Didacticism and moral uplift were a chief characteristic of both. The issue of the elderly's place in the structure of the family, however, leads toward later studies in human social organization, such as W. I. Thomas's work with Polish peasants and Conrad Arensberg's analyses of Irish rural life.

Another factor militating against early foundation interest in the elderly was their lack of visibility in urban settings. The truth was that the youthful sector of the American population had migrated steadily to metropolitan centers in search of industrial employment. This urban migration of the young was often accompanied by a rural retention of the elderly. Farm life maintained independence and staved off retirement. Remaining members of the rural family could also be relied upon for support whenever agricultural activity or health declined (Achenbaum, 1978:89). The evidence confronting the early foundation trustees indicated that the great majority of employed males were clustered in rural families at the turn of the century (Table 4.1). Further, the proportion of older adults in the population as a whole rose only slightly during the first three decades of foundation and university growth (Table 4.2). If the early foundations were reactive in spirit and in effort, they were clearly responding to the dubious metropolitan contributions of modernization. In the city itself, the aged constituted a limited and barely visible marker within a more tangible field of pressing urban images.

Contemporary studies of the elderly in rural environments were few but influential. Thomas's work on Polish peasants in Europe and America highlighted the strength of the aged's relationships with other family members both abroad and in American cities (Lopata, 1964). Moreover, such studies indicated clearly that the elderly retained a dignified and prized place within the family and within the community. That this pattern did not vary according to culture or nationality was vividly depicted in Conrad Arensberg's *The Irish Countryman*, first published in 1936. The elderly were a prominent feature of Irish life. This was particularly the case in rural areas that had witnessed a massive emigration of the young. Not only were the absolute numbers of elders in rural occupations higher than those in commerce or the professions, but also comparatively fewer elders on the farms were retired from gainful activity. Demographic studies indicated that even in the 1920s, Ireland had a higher proportion of adults over sixty-five years of age than the United States or Australia, major countries of immigration (Table 4.3).

What is striking in Arensberg's classic study, however, is the way in which analyses of intergenerational relationships show the elderly to be an integral, valued part of the community and inseparable from prevalent patterns of work or socializing. Older

Table 4.1
Employed Male Population in 1900, by Occupational Sector, Origin, and Ethnicity

Selected Employment Sectors	Native/White	Immigrant White	Black
Manufacturing	11.7%	16.6%	5.8%
Trade/Transportation	8.6%	8.4%	2.6%
Domestic Service/Personal Service	5.0%	10.0%	17.1%
Professions	3.9%	1.7%	0.7%
Agriculture	40.4%	25.4%	58.7%
All Sectors	69.7%	62.1%	84.9%

Source: Achenbaum (1978:97).
Note: Does not include women or white males of immigrant parents.

Table 4.2
Proportion of Adults over Sixty-five Years to the General U.S. Population, by Sex and Decade, 1890–1920

	Male	Female
1890	3.8%	3.8%
1900	4.0%	4.1%
1910	4.2%	4.4%
1920	4.6%	4.7%

Source: Derived from Achenbaum (1978:91).

people were the classical anthropological purveyors of traditional lore in its mythic, technical, and agricultural aspects. For this contribution, they received both "privilege and precedence." Regularly organized social groups that met in specific farmsteads in the evenings formed gathering places for older men

Table 4.3
Percentage in Population of Adults over Sixty-five in Selected Countries, 1926

Country	Older Adult Population %
United States	4.7%
Australia	4.4%
Germany	5.7%
England/Wales	6.6%
Sweden	8.8%
Ireland	9.2%

Source: Arensberg and Kimball (1968:160).

who discussed the character of relationships with other communities and slowly decided on whether to assimilate newer farming methods into older economic lifeways. The young attached themselves to such cliques of elders but were "listeners," without much of a voice or prestige, until a lucky one inherited his own small farm and the elderly parents moved to a revered place in a special "magical" part of the home. Importantly, the elderly were an integrating force in the rural communities of Ireland. Arensberg and Kimball (1968) wrote in a review of the earlier data, "The activities of the young men unite them across family. . . . But those of the old men do more; they unite the young and old as well" (p. 190).

In view of the early foundation attempt to provide skilled interventions for the purpose of social reform, the available evidence on the status of the elderly did not provide a sufficient basis for that rare and critical opportunity the more sizable foundation door was supposed to be open to. Far more critical seemed the need for educational reform and a concerted attack on infectious diseases and related problems of public health. Unemployment and underemployment among young urban workers and delinquency among the still more youthful were carefully documented by urban sociologists before foundation research monies were available. The need for a restructuring of old-age dependency relations from the family to public mechanisms of support was, moreover, not at all apparent. Indeed, existent studies of the elderly stressed a predominantly independent lifestyle and the presence of kinship ties that joined the aged to farm, family, and community in a positive way.

Still other contributions from the social sciences and social work may have inhibited a tendency for the early foundation trustees to view old age as a target for philanthropic support. For example, as social work grew more professional, it also grew increasingly reticent to include the elderly in clinical interventions. This reticence stemmed not from a lack of concern but rather from a negative appraisal of the aged in reigning psychiatric theory. To benefit from the therapeutic process, it was believed that a person had to be under fifty years of age; people under this age retained a mental "plasticity" (Kalosieh and Pedoto, 1989). Even Mary Richmond's emphasis on treatment informed by environmental understandings had by 1917 shown a considerable tilt toward psychodynamic infusions as well (Lubove, 1974:83). Though based on test results derived from laboratory animals, the contemporary studies of the learning capacity of older adults nevertheless "proved" that the elderly had little mental room for maneuver (Achenbaum, 1978:111). These ideas persisted even in the face of social research that had demonstrated that a rigorous and resilient old age was possible.

It was only in the 1930s with the Carnegie Foundation's turn toward adult learning that we find a cautious but growing attention to old-age issues in social work practice and in the social science literature. In 1930, the Deutsh Foundation, a smaller fund, underwrote a seminal conference on the elderly. This was soon followed by a lecture series for engaged professionals in 1937 sponsored by the New York Committee on Mental Hygiene.[3] However, no specialized course work on aging in the social sciences and social work appeared until the late 1950s, when combined support from the Ford Foundation, the Public Welfare Association, and the National Institute of Mental Health contributed to the development of a curriculum design in aging studies.

Foundation interest in aging studies between 1930 and 1960 was predominantly sporadic. Yet bibliographic sources highlight that at least two landmarks in the field—the one organizational, the other intellectual—occurred in 1945. Despite a lack of foundation support, therefore, some scholarly activity had been under way and was of sufficient quality to see the light of day. In 1945 Leo Simmons's classic cross-cultural study of aging in traditional societies was published.[4] The same year saw the founding of the Gerontological Society, which produced two still-dominant scientific journals, *Gerontologist* and *Journal of Gerontology*.

In the forty years between the 1920s and the 1960s, the foundation life of the nation remained peripheral to a growing scholarly interest in an expanding older adult population. The interest of the federal government was decidedly less marginal. In the 1940s the Public Health Service, later to be called the National Institutes of Health, set up a special unit that systematically reviewed existent biomedical and sociocultural research on the aged. Plans for the sponsorship of research were also set in motion (Achenbaum, 1978:141). A White House Conference on Aging followed in 1961 and signaled the government's growing engagement in old-age policy. From that time on, the public purse assumed a primary role in the endowment of research in the field of aging studies. This support may have seemed insufficient for a growing and healthy research enterprise, but it was available nonetheless. This support also complemented the major foundations' early emphasis on university growth and academic specialization. The academic base of sociology, anthropology, and social work was well established before federal monies for gerontology research were released.

The emergence of Aging Studies in the social sciences and social work evolved in a relatively cash-poor research environment. Nevertheless, it was an environment that increasingly recognized growing older-adult population problems of housing and health, issues surrounding age-linked illnesses, and a need for an understanding of the universals of the aging process as these could be uncovered through cross-cultural comparisons. One way to measure the growth of aging studies as a subfield within the social sciences and social work is to analyze patterns of Ph.D. productivity. The production of doctoral-level researchers whose theses have focused on gerontology is a good indicator of increased academic interest and can yield estimates of the availability of trained professionals in the light of educational, community, and national needs (Moore and Birren, 1971:249). A review of trends in doctoral productivity within social gerontology may also form a framework for foundation grant making by helping to make the growth of a significant academic subfield more visible to the foundation community.

Between 1930 and the early 1960s there was little actual expansion of Ph.D. production within social gerontology (Table 4.4). Moreover, this limited pattern of doctoral productivity occurred largely at Columbia and Chicago or at other institutions of higher learning where the foundation influence on the development of academic life had been significant (Table 4.5). Although the absolute number of universities graduating gerontology doctorates has now increased, this clustering within only certain university hands has continued into the 1980s.

Table 4.4
Area Study Gerontology in the Social Sciences: Ph.D. Productivity by Year, 1934–1966

Year	Total Ph.D's	% Gerontology Ph.D's
1934	606	1
1938	719	2
1942	846	1
1946	517	2
1950	1,186	7
1954	2,162	9
1958	2,365	10
1962	3,133	12
1966	4,517	19

Source: Derived from Moore and Birren (1971:250).
Note: "Social sciences" here and in the Moore and Birren table includes doctoral dissertations on religion, education, and physical education where theses topics had an aging focus.

From 1963 to 1985, Aging Studies in the social sciences and social work grew to 6 percent of all the doctorates produced in these fields (Table 4.6). Aging studies within social work seem to have grown most rapidly, while gerontology theses in anthropology represented only 3 percent of this discipline's doctorates. More refined patterns of Ph.D. productivity in social gerontology are best seen in the light of shorter time segments (Tables 4.7 and 4.8). For example, the total number of doctorates in the field of social work increased into the 1970s and then declined. In contrast, gerontology Ph.D.s within social work declined in the 1970s but rose gradually in the 1980s. Sociology reflected a dissimilar pattern. Aging Studies consistently managed to carve out a substantial niche at the doctoral level even though the total

Table 4.5
Ph.D. Productivity in Aging Studies at Selected Universities by
Total Number of Dissertations, 1934–1969 (N=81)

Significant Producers*	No. Dissertations
University of Chicago	40
Columbia University	36
New York University	30
University of Wisconsin	24
University of Southern California	23
Cornell University	23
Washington University (St. Louis)	22
University of Illinois	20
University of Minnesota	20
Berkeley	19
University of Michigan	18
Ohio State	17
University of Pennsylvania	15
Purdue	15
Columbia Teacher's College	14
Boston University	14
Iowa State University	14
University of Pittsburgh	12
Case Western Reserve	11

Source: Moore and Birren, 1971: 252.
Note: Significant Ph.D.-producing universities in Aging Studies are those together producing 50 percent or more of all Ph.D.s of the time period (707). Includes biomedical, psychology, and social science doctorates.

number of sociology doctorates expanded rapidly through the years as well. Overall doctoral productivity within anthropology fell off strikingly in the 1980s. Despite this decline, however, anthropological gerontology showed a measured growth.

It would be impossible in this context to discuss adequately all of the factors intimately involved in molding Ph.D. productivity over the past twenty years. Other studies of doctoral productivity have indicated that a carefully constructed analysis would include a survey of demographic trends, college course enrollments, faculty retention and attrition rates, and a host of additional factors involving university growth and development (D'Andrade et al., 1975). A preliminary discussion of supply and demand factors in social gerontology growth is presented in the following chapter in relation to program and curriculum is-

Table 4.6
Area Study Gerontology Ph.D.s in Anthropology, Sociology, and Social Work as a Proportion of Disciplinary Ph.D.s, 1963–1985

Discipline	Total No. Ph.D.'s 1963-1985	No. Area Gerontology Ph.D.'s 1963-1985	Gerontology Ph.D.'s, % Total
Anthropology	3,094	94	3.0%
Sociology	5,912	380	6.4%
Social Work	1,751	172	9.8%
Total	10,757	646	6.0%

Source: Calculated from *American Doctoral Dissertations* and *Dissertation Abstracts*. Anthropology here and in the text refers only to cultural anthropology and not to those subfields of the discipline, paleoanthropology or linguistics, whose contributions to Aging Studies have been comparatively and numerically minor in the light of the growing number of works stressing the sociocultural organization of aging and the aging process.

Note: 1963 has been taken as a base point for discussion since social work dissertations began to be cataloged for general reference in that year.

Table 4.7
Area Study Gerontology Ph.D.s as a Proportion of All Anthropology, Sociology, and Social Work Doctorates, 1963–1985, by Time Period ($N = 10,757$)

	I 1963–1967	II 1968–1973	III 1974–1979	IV 1980–1985
Anthropology	0.2%	2.3%	1.6%	2.6%
Sociology	1.2%	0.4%	3.6%	6.0%
Social Work	5.9%	1.6%	4.4%	5.5%

Source: American Doctoral Dissertations and Dissertation Abstracts, University Microfilms, Ann Arbor, Michigan.

Table 4.8
Doctoral Productivity in Anthropology, Sociology, and Social Work, 1963–1985

	Anthropology	Sociology	Social Work
1963–1967	239	1,267	184
% Gerontology	0.2	1.2	5.9
1968–1973	782	1,896	364
% Gerontology	2.3	0.4	1.6
1974–1979	1,650	1,599	785
% Gerontology	1.6	3.6	4.4
1980–1985	423	1,150	418
% Gerontology	2.6	6.0	5.5
Total	3,094	5,912	1,751

Source: Calculated from *American Doctoral Dissertations* and *Dissertation Abstracts*.
Note: Percentages do not sum to 100 due to rounding.

sues. At the moment it is sufficient to suggest that there is little relation between the overall level of doctoral productivity in the social sciences and social work and the production of gerontology Ph.D.s within these disciplines. Indeed, if increased social gerontology work at the doctoral level is taken not only as a reflection of statistics but also as a sign of a mutuality of interest and concern, then Aging Studies may have begun an academic life of its own. Such an academic definition means, among other things, that the subfield is becoming increasingly responsive to its own intellectual interests and to its own associational ties. It also implies that the future of gerontology studies within the social sciences and social work will become increasingly dependent on other institutional factors such as the academic job market and the relative availability of monies for research.

The growth of Aging Studies within the social sciences and social work may also be reviewed in the light of their acceptance within the university community (Table 4.9). In 1965 only 4 percent of American universities produced researchers with doctorates in social gerontology. Twenty years later, that number had climbed to 26 percent. Table 4.10, however, clearly indicates that doctorates in social gerontology were produced largely at a few major universities. Brandeis and Columbia were outstanding in this regard. At least 25 percent of gerontology Ph.D.s in the social sciences and social work were nevertheless obtained at an additional eighty-four universities. This healthy distribution im-

Table 4.9
Social Gerontology Ph.D.-Producing Universities as a Proportion of All Doctoral Producers, by Year

Year	No. Universities	% with area focus social Gerontology Ph.D.'s
1965	191	4% (8)
1975	244	8% (20)
1985	277	26% (72)

Source: *American Doctoral Dissertations*, University Microfilms, Ann Arbor, Michigan.

Table 4.10
Selected Universities as Significant Social Gerontology Ph.D. Producers, 1963–1985

University	No. Social Gerontology Ph.D.'s
Brandeis	26
Columbia	22
Michigan	16
Wisconsin-Madison	12
Univ. of Southern California	9
Case Western Reserve	9
Berkeley	8
Syracuse	8
UCLA-San Frarcisco	8
Northwestern	7
Cornell	7
Boston	7
Arizona	6
UCLA-LA	6
Utah	6
Minnesota	6

Source: American Doctoral Dissertations.
Note: The total number of doctorates in social gerontology in the time period surveyed was 646. Significant producers are those generating 1 percent or more of the total.

plies that a range of research precedents is being established and that these precedents can be creatively built upon by future doctoral candidates.

Dissertation topics within social gerontology exhibited an equally broad range of interests (Table 4.11), including the character of retirement communities and questions concerning self-concept and self-worth among the elderly. Social workers, however, showed a sharper focus on health service delivery mechanisms than gerontology Ph.D.s within anthropology or sociology. For their part, anthropologists interested in Aging Studies demonstrated an expected concentration on the ethnic and minority elderly (Table 4.12). Nearly 30 percent of all gerontology doctorates in anthropology devoted themselves to the nature of aging and the aging process among social and cultural minorities; only 7 percent of gerontology doctorates within sociology and social work had a similar focus. These data thus suggest that the study of the ethnic elderly might need to be more equitably distributed among social workers, sociologists, and anthropologists. The data also indicate that for the next few years, a clarification of the cultural molding of self-concept and of the character of social supports in later life will spring directly from anthropological encounters with the elderly despite anthropology's restrained doctoral productivity in Aging Studies.

A discussion of Ph.D. productivity in academic gerontology would be incomplete without underscoring the paucity of dissertation funding that underlay the launching of many researchers' careers. Additionally, the influence of inadequate research supports on choice of research topic and methodology needs to be examined briefly. In this respect, the Ford Foundation's[5] efforts to provoke the development of scholarship in Cross-Cultural or International Studies in the 1960s and 1970s felicitously affected anthropologists and comparative sociologists. McCaughey has reported that in the sixteen major universities he surveyed, theses with a cross-national or international focus rose from 22 percent to 30 percent of the total number of doctorates produced between 1966 and 1980 (1984:246–247).

The Ford Foundation's funding to International Studies, however, declined dramatically in the 1980s following a period of spurious reasoning that came to equate an apparent surfeit of International Studies doctorates with a surfeit of research on international subjects. It was predictable that anthropology would suffer a setback in doctoral productivity. Yet to a certain extent, many younger anthropologists rose to the challenge of a bleak funding future and adjusted to a lack of support for travel and extended on-site residence by shifting to ethnographic work that was carried out closer to home. In spite of a drastic impact on the discipline as a whole, therefore, Aging Studies in anthropology may have benefited from an ethnographic focus on urban neighborhoods and retirement communities.

A survey of dissertation topics in social gerontology nevertheless indicates the benefits anthropological gerontology gained from working in an American context did not necessarily outweigh significant losses stemming from trenchant cutbacks in International Studies funding. Nor did social gerontology in general profit from the insufficient underwriting of research on the part of both foundations and federal agencies. Gerontology researchers in anthropology, sociology, and social work have shown a similar attachment to studies of the support networks of the elderly, the character of familial ties, and the structure of retirement communities (Osgood, 1989; Silverman, 1987). Yet such work has received only a modest showing among topics chosen for dissertation research. One reason for this disparity between research interest and actual project is that such topics require advanced field methods, on-site surveys and residence, and return visits accompanied by updated evaluations. Extensive research monies are an adjunct of these methodologies and would seem to demand supports far in excess of those associated with attitudinal surveys conducted through the mails or social policy studies that can be derived from archival materials and census tracts. In those cases where a modest amount of on-site work was included in dissertation development, social work doctorates with a focus on aging studies might have had an advantage in being able to draw on academic affiliations linked with administrative settings. Even without much research funding, social work Ph.D.s were prominent where dissertation work in social gerontology addressed questions of institutionalization and health service delivery.

Table 4.11
Percentage Distribution of Significant Social Gerontology Theses Topics, by Discipline, 1963–1985 (N= 482)

Topic	Total Ph.D.'s	Anthropology	Sociology	Social Work
Housing/Community Environments	13%	15%	14%	8%
Health Services	13%	12%	11%	21%
Self Concept	13%	16%	13%	8%
Institutionalization	8%	4%	7%	13%
Social/Public Policy	7%	1%	3%	18%

Adjustment/Status Change	5%	9%	4%	3%
Social Supports/Networks	5%	4%	4%	9%
Work Force Issues	5%	1%	6%	5%
Death/Dying/Hospice	4%	9%	3%	1%
Retirement Communities	3%	3%	4%	—
Intergenerational Ties	1%	12%	11%	7%
General Retirement Issues	14%	12%	17%	5%

Source: *American Doctoral Dissertations*, and Moore and Birren surveys in the *Journal of Gerontology*, 1971 onward. Total does not sum to 100 due to rounding.

Note: "Significant" is defined as 1 percent or more Ph.D.s per topic and encompasses 75 percent of all Ph.D.s surveyed.

Table 4.12
Representation of Minority, Ethnic, and Cross-Cultural Studies in Area-Focus Gerontology Ph.D.s, by Academic Discipline, 1963–1985

Discipline	Total No. Ph.D.'s	Minority	Ethnic	Cross-Cultural
Anthropology	94	14 (15%)	4 (4%)	10 (9%)
Sociology	380	21 (5%)	4 (1%)	4 (1%)
Social Work	172	13 (7%)	–	–
Total	646			

Source: Calculated from *American Doctoral Dissertations* and *Dissertation Abstracts*.
Note: "Minority" is defined as a people of color; ethnic groups are defined as those who identify themselves and are identified by the broader society as distinctive of origin, civilization, religion, or language. The term "cross-cultural" encompasses comparative studies of two or more of the above either in the United States or cross-nationally. These taxonomies are sociocultural and do not reflect income level.

A lack of philanthropic support for dissertation research in social gerontology therefore has not undermined a growth in doctoral productivity or the collection of data necessary to address a variety of questions linked to the expansion of Aging Studies. It is equally the case, however, that without consistent foundation funding, doctoral candidates may have been kept overly tied to the university armchair. For this reason, available dissertations in social gerontology do not evince any great tendency to ressurrect the close empirical studies of the pioneers of the 1920s and 1930s. Community studies of the elderly in the crossroad towns or in urban neighborhoods have not been reclaimed for review and reevaluation. Nor has increased Ph.D. productivity in social gerontology stressed the analysis of the nature of the bonds between young and old that weave these communities together. Studies of Ph.D. productivity are nonetheless limited by their emphasis on quantity rather than quality and by their inability to speak to the character of postdoctoral achievement. Moreover, the great majority of those who undertook doctoral work in gerontology over the past two decades were traveling a largely new and distinct academic path. Much can be said of the fact that working largely alone within specialized academic departments, they nevertheless converged decisively on the need for advanced inquiries into an issue essential to national policy and public decision making.

NOTES

1. Quoted in Kevles (1987:411).
2. Quoted in Young (1966:18) during a discussion of the apparent contemporary need to locate a pioneer in science history while ignoring contextual problems of conceptual development.
3. See Lowy's discussion of the history of the linkage between social work and Aging Studies in Lowy (1989).
4. See Simmons (1945).
5. The Ford Foundation was established in 1936.

5

Entering the Aging Mode: Social Gerontology and the Universities

> Among many social groups science as such enjoys something closer to toleration than reverence.
>
> Daniel Kevles (1987:xi)

Two further points need to be clarified with respect to Ph.D. productivity in social gerontology. One clarification involves a process of enclosure into the academy already referred to in a discussion of social work in the early twentieth century. If social work's enclosure into the university system has been incomplete due to its continuing ties to the voluntary sector, social gerontology does not seem to have experienced this process at all. Aging Studies grew up in already specialized academic fields, as well as in a limited number of prestigious universities. Rather than have moved in from the periphery of the academic world, social gerontology evolved at the center of university life and has gradually spread to smaller university systems.

A related clarification addresses itself to the retention of social gerontology as a research activity in the postdoctoral years. Bernard Barber has written that even in the time of efflorescent university growth, only 25 percent of those with doctoral degrees continued research after completing their doctoral studies (Barber, 1952:152). To what extent does a similar pattern of research retention exist within social gerontology today? Moreover, what is the relationship between social gerontology Ph.D.s and academic employment? At issue is not simply the well-known tension between teaching or research activity in the faculty community (Rossi, 1966). Also relevant is the tie between levels of Ph.D. productivity in social gerontology and an increasing demand for skilled instructors in the field of Aging Studies.

A preliminary survey of scholars who wrote theses in social gerontology indicates that their postdoctoral research experience was highly oriented toward Aging Studies' issues (Table 5.1). Although continuing intellectual interest is a strong factor behind postdoctoral work in social gerontology, this retention of interest may itself be linked to academic employment (Table 5.2). Collegial relationships may well underlie the fact that the transition from doctoral to postdoctoral research saw no substantial decline in a concern for retirement and housing issues, as well as for the problems of the institutionalized aged (Table 5.3).

The relative availability of research supports also plays a role in the retention of social gerontology as a scholarly activity in the postdoctoral period (Tables 5.4 and 5.5). Between 1963 and 1985, dissertation funding fell mainly to federal agencies. Other mechanisms of fiscal support encompassed an intricate combination of smaller amounts of government monies with funds from other granting vehicles. Foundations provided only a highly restricted portion of the total support for social gerontology theses. Indeed, doctoral candidates remained a significant funding resource for their own dissertations. This pronounced self-financing of research appears almost as familiar in contemporary academic life as it did in the early days of social science growth.

Patterns of postdoctoral research funding in social gerontology did not diverge significantly from trends in predoctoral supports. The federal government, packaged funding, and self-support provided the greatest share of social gerontology research monies. The single departure from this pattern was the entrance onto the research funding scene of a small number of newer

Table 5.1
Percentage of Gerontology-Area-Focus Ph.D.s Pursuing Aging Research at Postdoctoral Level, by Discipline, 1963–1985

Discipline	No. Ph.D.'s	% Pursuing Post-Doctoral Aging Research
Anthropology	21	84%
Sociology	26	87%
Social Work	18	66%
Total	65	76.9%

Source: Author's survey.
Note: A one-third random sample of the 646 social gerontology doctorates was chosen for a questionnaire mailing. Respondent number is representative of 10 percent of the total doctoral productivity.

Table 5.2
Proportion Gerontology-Area-Focus Ph.D.s, 1963–1985, by Postdoctoral Gerontology Productivity and Employment Sphere (*N*=65)

	Anthropology	Sociology	Social Work
No. Gerontology Ph.D.'s	21	26	18
% in Post-Ph.D. Gerontology research Current Employment (%)	84%	87%	66%
Academic	61%	100%	73%
Government	–	–	2%
Foundation	–	–	–
*Independent/ Voluntary Sector	38%	–	15%
Private Clinician	–	–	10%

Source: Author's survey.
Note: The category of "independent/voluntary sector" includes independent researchers and private consultants to the voluntary and private sectors, as well as voluntary agency personnel.

Table 5.3
Distribution of Doctoral and Postdoctoral Research Topics in Social Gerontology, 1963–1985 (N = 50)

Topic	Dissertation Distribution	Post-Doctoral Distribution
Health/H. Services	8%	30%
Retirement Issues	13%	12%
Housing/Community		
Environments	8%	10%
Self-Concept	10%	8%
Institutionalization	5%	5%
Adjustment/Status Change	8%	6%
Retirement Communities	8%	6%
Intergenerational Ties	16%	6%
Social Policy	5%	4%
Workforce	5%	4%
Death/Dying/Hospice	2%	4%
Social Supports	5%	–
Uncategorized	2%	–

Source: Author's survey.

Table 5.4
Funding Sources of Ph.D. Theses in Social Gerontology, 1963–1985
($N=65$)

Single Source	% of Total
Government Agency	36%
None (Personal Funds)	15%
General Purpose Foundation	8%
University Funds	8%
Aging-Specific Foundation	1%
Multiple Source Funding*	32%

Source: Author's survey.
*Involves "packaged" funding on the investigators' part and includes two or more of the single-source funding components.

Table 5.5
Postdoctoral Aging Research Funding in Anthropology, Sociology, and Social Work, 1963–1985 ($N=65$)

Single Source	% of Projects
Government	35%
None (Personal Funds)	14%
University Funds	13%
General Purpose Foundation	8%
Aging-Specific Foundation	8%
Multiple Source Funding	21%

Source: Author's survey.

aging-specific foundations whose capacity to fund research was welcome but restrained.

If there has been a variety of sources for research monies in social gerontology, there has also been a prominent need to rely on packaged funding, where small amounts are pooled from diverse granting mechanisms in order to arrive at an amount appropriate to affect research goals. Self-financing is a critical part of packaged research funding, and the constrained amounts involved in these supports may have favored studies utilizing mailings or archival materials. Studies encompassing travel, community residence, and the testing of interview materials in the light of behavioral observations may have been forgone for issues of cost and cost-effectiveness. Even in the postdoctoral period, therefore, there has been little tendency for scholars to reclaim an earlier twentieth-century interest in assessing the role of the elderly in community activity and integration. The process of confronting "old people as people," however, requires an evaluation of the realities of behavior in specific settings, not only the mechanical perception of the elderly through the filter of a statistical table. The usage of community study methods in social gerontology may have been limited not only by the growing diversity of interests in the field but also by underdeveloped research supports and the existence of highly preliminary public and private grant-making vehicles.

Given a growing faculty that is specialized in social gerontology, what factors in the structure of American institutions of higher learning are acting to support this faculty's development and growth?[1] One factor that leads to an increasing demand for social gerontology faculty is the impressive growth in Aging Studies course work over the last three decades. Gerontology instruction is now available at community colleges, in undergraduate programs, and at the graduate level as well (Table 5.6). A great number of gerontology instructional programs are formalized and offer students a certificate, undergraduate or graduate degree, or other evidence of specialized work. The historical underpinnings of the gerontology presence on American campuses date to the late 1940s. By 1957, 57 American campuses had some instruction in gerontology. In the 1980s that number had grown

Table 5.6
Academic or Organizational Units of Gerontology Instruction, 1986

Unit	No.	No. campuses %
Program	155	38.4%
Center	72	17.8%
Institute	29	7.2%
Department	23	5.7%
Committee	14	3.5%
Division	13	3.2%
Uncategorized	98	24.3%

Source: Adapted from Peterson (1986–1987: Table 1).

to 1,071, and gerontology instruction itself seemed increasingly clustered at larger university systems that offer graduate education and advanced degrees (Table 5.7). Faculty involvement in gerontology instruction has similarly expanded and now includes 6,000 instructors. This number is substantial but far exceeds the number of doctoral-level social gerontology researchers and instructors who have entered into academic life over the past two decades. The available literature thus suggests that the need for instructors in gerontology within American university systems might be growing at a faster rate than the production of appropriately trained academic specialists.

Another factor that supports faculty development in social gerontology is the growing number of courses in the fields of anthropology, sociology, and social work now included in gerontology programming. At the undergraduate level of gerontology instruction, sociology exhibits a large and extensive representation in programs offering a degree or certificate in gerontology.[2] Social work courses are present in at least one-third of formal gerontology programs at the undergraduate level, though an-

Table 5.7
Type of Degree and Credentialing in Gerontology on American Campuses, 1986.

Degree	No. of Campuses
Bachelor's	20
Minor	26
Concentration	12
Certificate	62
Master's	19
Minor	2
Concentration	12
Certificate	49
Doctorate	1
Minor	1
Concentration	2
Certificate	3

Source: Adapted from Peterson (1987: Table 1).

thropology courses are offered in only 17 percent of such formal gerontology instructional units (Table 5.8).

At the level of graduate work in Aging Studies, sociology and social work course work is present at even higher levels than in undergraduate gerontology programs. This same trend is present with respect to course work in anthropology, which enjoys a marked rise in gerontology programming associated with graduate degrees (Table 5.9). It is probable that the field of sociology figures so prominently in gerontology instructional units

Table 5.8
Percentage Representation of Disciplinary Course Work in Undergraduate Gerontology Programs, 1985 (N=63)

Department/Area Course	% in Undergraduate Gerontology
Sociology	77%
Psychology	66%
Biology	57%
Social Work	33%
Physical Education	30%
Home Economics	27%
Nursing	25%
Economics	25%
Education	23%
Counseling	20%
Health/Nutrition	19%
Administration	17%
Anthropology	17%

Source: Sullivan (1985).
Note: Includes B.A. degree with major, minor, certificate, or concentration. Disciplines with 10 percent or more representation within sixty-three programs are listed.

Table 5.9
Percentage Representation of Disciplinary Course Work in Graduate Gerontology Programs, 1985 (N=72)

Department/Area Course	% in Graduate Gerontology Programs
Sociology	94%
Psychology	72%
Biology	47%
Social Work	47%
Education	45%
Nursing	36%
Anthropology	36%
Physical Education	32%
Home Economics	22%
Counseling	22%
Health/Nutrition	20%
Speech	18%
Administration	15%

Source: Sullivan (1985).
Note: Includes M.A. degree with major, minor, certificate, or concentration. Disciplines with 10 percent or more representation within seventy-two programs are listed.

because of its lengthy history of interest in Aging Studies. The decisive presence of social work at the graduate level may be traced in part to the fact that many gerontology programs are able to draw on instructors and curriculum materials already linked to social work education in graduate social work faculties. Anthropology's lower representation in gerontology programs may be accounted for by a variety of factors, including a lesser degree of disciplinary visibility than sociology and social work. Many smaller and modestly endowed colleges lack anthropology departments; much course work in anthropology is still taught by sociologists. Moreover, there remains a continuing suspicion that much of anthropology consists of no more than a series of uncoordinated, unrelated facts about foreign cultures; such exotica are considered inappropriate to gerontology training for service delivery to an older and essentially postindustrial population (Hornum and Glascock, 1989). That this suspicion has been somewhat allayed is evident in the significant rise in anthropology course work available to students of gerontology at the graduate level. Anthropological gerontology has seen a measured growth over the past two decades. It is therefore probable that an increasing penetration of anthropological concepts surrounding aging and the aging process will continue to be welcomed into the gerontology curriculum as research in anthropological gerontology expands and matures.

An additional factor underlying a need for gerontology faculty is the character of legislative activity at the federal level. This activity has not only provoked a demand for gerontology researchers; it has also underscored a growing need for clinical specialists of interdisciplinary training.[3] Higher education has responded with what Peterson refers to as an almost invisible development of gerontology instruction. Gerontology programming has evolved within university systems with little federal or foundation support. Indeed, any student of this underfinanced but successful academic growth is forced to echo Peterson's conclusion that the development of gerontology instruction has occurred largely as a "response to the aging of society and a recognition that gerontology is an important instructional area" (Peterson, 1986).

In order to estimate the actual need for doctoral-level social gerontologists in the light of increased academic opportunity, we would have to look closely at the nature of college and university enrollments, student-faculty ratios, and the character of postdoctoral movement into Aging Studies' research on the part of established university faculty. Although these factors must remain unexamined, it is still possible to project that gerontology programs and instruction will continue to expand throughout American institutions of higher education. I would not go so far as to state that the turn of the century will witness the advent of gerontology instruction on every American campus (Peterson, 1986), yet there is no doubt that the university has seen the "coming of age." It may be expected, therefore, that both predoctoral and postdoctoral researchers in social gerontology will continue to find a growing level of academic activity and opportunity on American campuses in the future.

It is anticipated that an increased growth in gerontology instruction will bring with it an increased demand for research funding. In this respect, the rise of gerontology programs in higher education occurred largely outside the contemporary foundation agenda. Social gerontology research activity would seem to require its own rightful place in foundation life if universities are to continue to provide a sophisticated academic context for the education of a growing number of students who are choosing the field of Aging Studies for a liberal arts major, graduate work, or professional career.

In view of the major foundations' early twentieth-century emphasis on university and faculty development, it seems ironic that contemporary foundation work should show only constrained financial commitments to academic gerontology. One of the more compelling reasons behind a reticence to invest in the academic growth of gerontology lies in a series of chastening foundation experiences with other interdisciplinary fields. Analysts of trends in higher education began to raise serious questions about Ph.D. productivity in relation to institutional demands as far back as the 1950s. A belief that a shortage of doctoral degree holders was at hand seemed to be effectively confirmed by the prevailing habit of equating the "qualified" university teachers with those who held the doctoral degree. Additional confirmation was found in a set of labor statistics that indicated that only 40 percent of university faculty actually possessed the advanced degree (McCaughey, 1984:173-176). Although data collected in the 1960s pointed to a burgeoning level of Ph.D. productivity, the shortage issue remained a vital and successful technique for attracting foundation monies to academic projects. Foundations reacted to the Ph.D. shortfall issue with enthusiasm. Apparently they also responded overenthusiastically to "shortages" in the field of International Studies, an interdisciplinary area of study that includes both the social sciences and the humanities. At least one historian has noted that the field of International Studies may have been "saturated" with doctoral holders long before foundations actively noticed a Ph.D. oversupply (McCaughey, 1984).

The interdisciplinary field of Women's Studies has been a more recent entry point for foundation supports. The growing problem with this area seems less a question of saturation than how to get the field to the point of saturation if the public interest cannot be maintained. Despite a growth of women's centers, specialized institutes, and Women's Studies programs on university campuses, there is still no permanency in Women's Studies faculty (Stimpson and Cobb, 1986:21,57). Whether foundations should continue to help the expansion of permanent instructional units in Women's Studies remains an important question for contemporary philanthropic management. Foundation supports to research *on* women represents one funding direction. Continuing support for the expansion of academic programs involving course work and research *in* the specialized field of Women's Studies is another distinct process with a different outcome. Today birthrates are declining, there is a predictable shrinkage in undergraduate enrollments, and women, the primary student cadre in Women's Studies programs, are growing more oriented toward professional careers. It is not known in what way these trends will influence the expansion or contraction of Women's Studies programs on university campuses. It seems reasonable to assume, however, that there will be only a limited number of women who will continue to seek out academic programs where they are considered as a relatively discrete topic of study. A more appropriate avenue for foundation generosity might lie in the support of academic programs in which women can attain the generic skills they will need in order to adapt to complex social organizations after graduation.

The foundation role in International Studies growth was a response to critical societal conditions. Although levels of Ph.D. "saturation" may have been reached by the 1970s, foundations nevertheless supported the education of specialists who could clarify significant socioeconomic changes following the expansion of the American economy and political value system after World War II. It is not so certain that Women's Studies will now exhibit the type of academic expansion experienced by the International Studies community in a different historical context. Foundation support for Women's Studies has not come totally in reaction to critical structural changes in society. Rather, philanthropic trusts such as the Ford, Mellon, and Eli Lilly foundations have engaged in one of our more dubious contemporary customs and have responded only to those public coalitions with the loudest voice and the best ability to filter public opinion. That the opinions of the majority of people may have been filtered out of this foundation engagement with Women's Studies is reflected in the dilatory growth of specialized programs, academic departments, and degree-awarding institutions. Major foundations therefore have tended to confuse strength of advocacy with a need for the clarification of a complex subject matter within formal academic structures.

It would be fair to state that academic social gerontology has evolved without the aid of advocates and without any public agitation on its behalf. Indeed, the growth of gerontology programs in American universities has arisen without extensive fiscal supports and as a direct and decisive response to an increasingly older population and an associated demand for trained researchers and clinical gerontologists. If foundations have a notable tendency to commit too many "large masses of property to unalterable uses" (Fosdick, 1964:193), they also have the flexibility to shift directions in the face of a legitimate need. One legitimate need that must be met in the field of Aging Studies is an increase of trained, doctoral-level faculty. A large proportion of gerontology students have an immediate occupational orientation (Peterson, 1987). Moreover, the study of aging and the aging process remains a subfield of other academic disciplines and is without its own Ph.D.-awarding departments. Since the great majority of students now engaged in gerontology work will not advance to a research degree, Ph.D. replenishments must come from two sources. One potential pool of gerontology instructors consists of those university faculty without a gerontology Ph.D. who have undertaken research on aging in the postdoctoral period. A smaller pool of gerontology faculty comprehends scholars whose doctoral theses involved gerontological subjects. As we have seen with respect to social gerontology, this group of faculty consists of only 6 percent of the Ph.D.s produced in the social sciences and social work between 1963 and 1985. Course work in the social sciences and social work today constitutes an integral part of the gerontology curriculum on an increasing number of American campuses. This potential pool of faculty thus seems highly limited and constrained given the need for quality faculty with a sophisticated gerontology background.

The interdisciplinary field of Women's Studies faces critical problems of development tied to the fluctuations of interest in its subject matter and doubts about its realistic applications to a variety of professional situations. In contrast, the social and cultural study of aging has evolved dramatically as a consequence of public and student interest, as well as from an increased need for health service professionals with a multidisciplinary background (Maynard and Shiffman, 1988). Foundation supports could facilitate the growing need for gerontology program enrichment on American college campuses. Foundation subventions for dissertation and postdoctoral research in social gerontology would help ease an increasing demand for doctoral-level university instructors. As student gerontologists will continue to seek professional careers outside of the university system, this demand might be expected to expand considerably in the coming decades.

NOTES

1. Except where indicated, this discussion is based on David Peterson's work (1986–1987, 1986, 1987). Gerontology as used by Peterson includes social gerontology as well as psychogerontology, education, and various fields within geriatrics.

2. Author's survey from E. Sullivan, ed. (1985).

3. See Parhan and Wood (1988) on federal legislative activity and the growth of education for gerontology.

6

The Calculus of Charity: Funding for Social Gerontology

> If you cannot measure, your knowledge is meagre and unsatisfactory.
>
> Lord Kelvin[1]
>
> If you cannot measure, measure anyhow.[2]
>
> Frank Knight (sociologist)

In the 1940s Vannevar Bush, a former dean at MIT and head of the Carnegie Institution, petulantly declared that he was "no scientist," just an "engineer."[3] This statement reflected a persistent academic partition between the theoretical and applied aspects of physics and might have been calculated to deflect an intense public perception that the physical sciences seemed to hold unsavory links to the military and to corporate enterprise. Social gerontology too contains its definite theoretical and practical components. These components, however, have been closely wedded in university programs in an effort to produce informed clinicians with multidisciplinary training. Moreover, the service delivery facets of social gerontology have tended to provoke popular appreciation and academic growth even in the face of discouraging support from the public and private sectors (Parhan and Wood, 1988). There thus exists no real public ambivalence toward the activities of gerontology specialists and little public questioning about a political hold over those engaged in Aging Studies. In contrast to other sciences in their emergent periods of growth, the science of aging has therefore suffered less from tensions between the nature of academic pursuits and the character of public opinion. Rather, it has enjoyed a measure of public recognition but a paucity of federal and philanthropic support.

It is not yet known how only constrained subventions from grant-making agencies have affected the process of discipline building in Aging Studies and among the collectivity of gerontology scholars. However, it may not be too premature to write that existent funding mechanisms have tended to favor biomedical concerns within gerontology studies rather than inquiries into the sociocultural organization of later life. This chapter looks at the manner in which foundation support for biogerontology research has nevertheless been accompanied by increased subventions to the establishment and maintenance of community service programs for the elderly. It is at the level of the local project or program that theoretical research in social gerontology can best join forces with the work of gerontology clinicians. This combined effort may prove a fruitful arena for future foundation grant giving.

In spite of the early foundations' prominent role in the development of higher education, the federal government quickly became the home of many of the nation's most eminent scientific entrepreneurs. After World War II, the government became the largest source of monies for academic science as well. The National Institute on Aging (NIA) was founded in 1974 as part of the National Institutes of Health (NIH). In 1985, at least 52 percent of all NIH awards, or $2 billion, went to the nation's medical schools, 23 percent of NIH monies was awarded to other educational institutions, and 19 percent was granted to nonprofit groups and to hospitals (NIH, 1987). The NIA budget in 1984 reflected the federal granting pattern, for a majority of its monies was clearly won by the geriatrics and biomedical fields (NIH, 1986; Table 6.1). Another federal agency, the Administration on Aging (AOA), has addressed issues concerning the relationships among the aging process, family and ethnic organization, and local community structures. These are issues that complement the NIA's smaller awards granted under its Older People and Society and Behavioral Sciences funding agenda. Available materials, however, indicate that between 1971 and 1981, university scholars received 58 percent of the rather limited number of AOA awards, or a total of eighty-six dispersions. The remainder of the grants were distributed among operating foundations and nonprofit corporations (AOA, 1982).

If grants from the NIA appear to be biomedically concentrated, AOA grants to social gerontology research seem to be targeted to a delimited number of geographic areas. The regional distribution of its grants shows that nearly 50 percent of agency grant monies went to institutions in California, Washington, D.C., New York, and Pennsylvania. The rest of the grants between 1979 and 1981 were widely dispersed over twenty-one states.

Table 6.1
Grant Distribution of NIA to Selected Areas in Gerontology, 1978 and 1984

	1978	1984
Molecular/Cell Biology	7,615	15,380
Physiology of Aging	8,777	29,421
Geriatrics	1,586	19,286
Older People and Society+	2,666	3,875

Source: NIH (1986:19). Dollars are in thousands.
+This category does not include grants targeted toward the psychosocial aspects of aging.

Each state received an average of only two social gerontology grants during those three years (AOA, 1982). The tendency for the federal government to concentrate science funding within a limited number of prestigious universities may be mirrored in the fact that high levels of Ph.D. productivity within social gerontology are confined to a relatively few institutions. Indeed, generic federal funding to science continues to reaffirm previously established ties to only 50 prominent universities out of the more than 200 in the American university system. Among these are those that generate intense numbers of dissertations in gerontology (Sommer, 1987:448). Moreover, since the 1960s, the federal government has strongly favored the funding of life-science research (Sommer, 1987). One outcome of such targeted dollars has been an increasing medicalization of aging research. Another obvious result has been that many creative studies in social gerontology were conceived and concluded in a research context characterized by shrunken fiscal supports. If the public has become bullish on social gerontology issues, the public purse has nevertheless remained decidedly timid.

Specialization in national granting agencies might also have contributed to contemporary disparities between biogerontology research supports and those granted to the social and cultural sciences. Anthropological and cross-cultural approaches to the aging process are often supported by the National Science Foundation (NSF) where a relatively few scientists may be involved in peer review and grant making (Sommer, 1987). Procedural considerations as well as a lack of exposure to diverse and emergent trends in the field may act to inhibit ventures in anthropological gerontology. Additionally, restrictions may be set to growing scholarly needs in the anthropology of aging relative to library and data-base costs or to expenses surrounding extensive travel and fieldwork.

Although the number of foundation grants to the aged rose in the 1980s, foundation interest in the elderly seems overshadowed by a focus on youth (Table 6.2). Nor has the federal tendency to medicalize aging research been offset by the grant-giving patterns of the major philanthropic trusts. This is true despite a growth in foundation giving to the elderly and for aging research since the 1970s (Table 6.3), and the appearance of

Table 6.2
Grants for Selected Population Groups by 444 Foundations, 1981 and 1985

Group	% of Grants 1981	% of Grants 1985	Four Year %
Aged	1.4	2.8	+1.4%
Children/Youth	9.8	10.7	+0.9%
Minorities	1.9	1.7	-0.2%
Women/Girls	2.9	4.0	+1.1%

Source: Foundation Grants Index, 15th ed. (1986: Table ID).
Note: Grants are for $5,000 or more from foundations with $1 million in assets/or granting $100,000 or more annually.

Table 6.3
Foundation Grant Making for Aging Projects and Research, by Foundation Type, 1976 and 1985

	Number of Foundations	
	1976	1985
Corporate	3	8
Community	2	5
Private	14	34

Source: Author's survey from Foundation Grants Index, 15th edition, 1986.

a number of foundations, including the Florence V. Burden and the Villers, that devote themselves exclusively to grant making for the elderly.

Foundation grant making to aging programs and research was nevertheless circumscribed and highly targeted to specific projects (Table 6.4). Both private and corporate foundations supported some gerontology research, but monies went primarily to biomedical endeavors. An interest in the social policy aspects of social gerontology was clear with respect to the grant-giving patterns of the private foundations but less intense in the work of corporate and community trusts.[4]

Program supports for the elderly favor those that train hospice and home health workers and the establishment of senior centers and institutional settings (Table 6.5). Foundations also evinced a concern for supporting home and housing complex equity in the case of retirement communities. There seems a real disparity between a pronounced foundation interest in biomedical research and a scant foundation underwriting of adult day care programs. Children of aged parents with Alzheimer's disease and other debilitating conditions are often overburdened by care services to their parents as well as to their younger children. With foundation support, a growth of adult day care centers would provide a setting for medical service delivery to the "frail" elderly while offering their midlife children an opportunity to continue normal daily activities. This lack of relationship be-

Table 6.4
Selected Foundation Giving to Aging Programs and Aging Research, by Foundation Type, 1984–1986

Type	Giving in Millions	% to Elderly	Programs	Medical Research	Nonmedical+ Research
Total	644	5.9	79.7	7.8	10.7
Private/ National	328	9.7	84.0	3.6	9.0
Private/ Limits	135	3.0	61.0	36.0	0.9
Community	86	1.2	100.0	–	–
Corporate	95	4.9	54.0	35.0	6.0

Source: Figures are derived from foundations listing giving to research and project development relative to older adults in Weiss and Mahlmann (1987).

+ An additional and smaller amount, or 4.6 percent of total foundation giving to the elderly and related research or policy evolution, went for the endowment of university chairs and toward institutional grants for conference and publications.

Table 6.5
Foundation Supports to Programs for the Elderly by Focus of Support, 1984

	No.	%	Average Grant
Homecare/Training And Services	13	19%	$13,000
Health/Hospice Programs	12	17%	$12,000
Senior Center Supports	12	17%	$ 7,000
Nursing Home Support	9	13%	$10,000
Housing Program Support	9	13%	$ 6,000
Employment Service	8	11%	$ 5,000
Adult Day Care	5	7%	$ 5,000

No. grants = 68

Source: Foundation Grants Index, 15th ed. (1986).
Note: Based on a 20 percent random sample within each granting category listed in the index irrespective of type of foundation. Percentages do not sum to 100 because of rounding.

tween foundation research and program funding may be taken as a sign of the fluid state that exists between philanthropic and social gerontology efforts today. More coordination among the many foundation projects in Aging Studies research and service delivery to the elderly might be one outcome of the growing tie between the philanthropic community and the elderly. This coordination does not imply a loss of resiliency in philanthropic management but rather a closer interplay between existing theoretical and programmatic endeavors that foundations have already chosen to support.

A review of scientific journal articles in the field of social gerontology may highlight the strength of federal funding from

1976 to 1986. Of fifty-three journal articles in social gerontology surveyed, over 64 percent contained research sponsored by federal agencies, while 22 percent were self-financed (Table 6.6). Foundations also sponsored research that ultimately appeared in scientific journal format, but at least 57 percent of philanthropic support emanated from the Andrus Foundation alone. Other significant foundation names, such as the Danforth, Robert Wood Johnson, Sloan, Hogg, Walgreen, and Ford and Rockefeller foundations, appear infrequently in author acknowledgments of research sponsors. Although the range of government agencies supporting social gerontology research was broad and offered scholars funding mechanisms other than those of the NIH and AOA, an emphasis on self-financed research continued to remain prominent (Table 6.7).

Whatever the ultimate source of funding, social gerontologists exhibited an overwhelming concern for the study of attitudes toward later life among the elderly, for the nature of intergenerational ties and support networks, and for issues surrounding retirement from the labor force (Table 6.8). Newer interests, such as hospitalization usage rates, victimization, and later-life mar-

Table 6.6
Funding Sources of Published Social Gerontology Studies, 1976–1986

Funding Source	Number of Projects
Single Source	34 (64.1%)
Dual Funding Source	5 (9.4%)
Multiple Funding Source	2 (3.7%)
(No Apparent Support)	(12) [22.6%]

Source: Derived from a survey of social science articles, 1976–1986, in *Journal of Gerontology*, calculated from even-numbered years and from articles listed under "Social and Behavioral Sciences." Only those articles authored or coauthored by those in the fields of sociology, anthropology, and/or social work were surveyed.

Table 6.7
Funding Agencies by Type: Single-Source Grants for Published Articles, 1976–1986 (N = 34)

Granting Agency	% Grants Funded
NIA	26.4%
AOA	23.5%
NIMH	14.7%
NSF	8.8%
*Other public agencies/one grant each	20.5%
Faculty Development Grant	5.8%

Source: Derived from a survey of social science articles, 1976–1986, in *Journal of Gerontology*.
Note: See Table 6.6 for survey procedures.
*DHHS, Health Care Financing Administration, Social Security Administration, U.S. Public Health, Urban Renewal Administration, NICHD

riages, have begun to supplement an earlier focus on institutionalization and housing patterns.

While the topics of journal articles were diverse, study methods were limited in scope and creativity. The majority of research reports were based on census tracts, regional and county surveys, and analyses of questionnaires sent through the mails (Table 6.9). If contact with the elderly or their family was a cardinal part of the study, study sites remained situated in the researcher's own place of residence or university employment.

I have written that methodologies were limited. This limitation does not necessarily lie in the fact that the majority of study methods involved attitudinal and other surveys ultimately meant for presentation in statistical form. Such studies are part of the traditional repertoire of the social sciences and provide a general backdrop for clinical work or policy formation. Social gerontology, however, is a repository of other significant tradi-

Table 6.8
Subject Matter of Published Articles in Social Gerontology, 1976–1986

Topic	No.	%
Self-Concept/Life Satisfaction	8	15.0%
Intergenerational Relationships	7	13.2%
Retirement Issues	5	9.4%
Support Networks	5	9.4%
Income Adequacy/Poverty	4	7.5%
Age Stratification	3	5.6%
Later Life Marriages	3	5.6%
Housing	3	5.6%
Clergy/Religion/Aged	3	5.6%
Institutionalization	3	5.6%
Longevity Studies	2	3.7%
Age/Activity	2	3.7%
Hospitalization	2	3.7%
Widowhood	1	1.8%
Victimization	1	1.8%
Uncategorized	1	1.8%

Source: Derived from *Journal of Gerontology*, 1976–1986.
Note: See Table 6.6 for survey procedures.

tions; these can surround attitudes and beliefs with empirical observations of actual behavior. At one point in foundation history, subventions to social science were sufficient to permit lengthy periods of fieldwork. Today a paucity of foundation funding has contributed to the emergence of the mailed survey

Table 6.9
Project Methods in Social Gerontology, by Participating Funding Agents, 1976–1986 (N = 53)

Project Methods	% Total	Sources of Funding		
		% Federal	% Foundation	% (No Funding)
Analyses: Census and Survey Data	43.4%	78.2%	13.0%	(8.6%)
Home Interviews: Scholar's Locality	28.3%	60.0%	6.6%	(33.3%)
Mailed Surveys/ Directory-Based	13.2%	16.6%	33.3%	(50.0%)
Neighborhood Studies: On-site Living	9.4%	80.0%	—	(20.0%)
Uncategorized/or Multi-Method	5.6%	66.6%	—	(33.3%)

Source: Derived from *Journal of Gerontology*, 1976–1986.
Note: See Table 6.6 for survey procedures.

and census tract analysis as a primary tool of social gerontology research. It is nevertheless difficult to ascertain whether the research presented in journal articles is representative of the field of social gerontology as a whole or has been published because materials are presented in an accepted editorial format. Over 37 percent of the articles, however, indicate that some on-site fieldwork has supplemented attitudinal surveys. It may also be suggested that social gerontology researchers might want to increase their amount of behaviorally based researches if these were underwritten by stronger funding supports. This suggestion can be partially clarified by another armchair survey of the research aspirations of social gerontologists who wrote Ph.D. theses in Aging Studies between the years 1963 and 1985 (Table 6.10).

An outstanding feature of the research desires of social gerontology Ph.D.s is a wish to undertake long-term studies of aging and the aging process in international contexts. A second research aspiration encompassed a need to reexamine the life of the rural elderly. In the days of the early foundations, rural areas were characterized by closely knit family networks and family-based support services for the elderly. These facets of rural life have largely passed and have given way to a growing need for external supports that derive from metropolitan centers. This does not mean that the rural elderly are isolated or that they do not maintain continuing links to the rural youth who have migrated to the city for employment (Buechler and Buechler, 1987). Inquiries into migration fields that wed countryside with city are an important component of the study of the rural elderly, yet such studies require more foundation and federal largesse than is now available.

A survey of research aspirations also indicates that the propensity to examine aging issues through the use of mailed questionnaires is still evident. Studies of volunteerism among the elderly are anticipated as well, especially where the elderly volunteer is involved with youth and other older adults. Mailed surveys that question administrators about health policy issues constitute another broad examination social gerontologists might want to undertake in the future. However, it seems unlikely that the acceptance of health services by the elderly, or their degree of

Table 6.10
Type of Postdoctoral Social Gerontology Projects Anticipated, by Methodology and Estimated Cost ($N = 42$)

Method	#	Estimated Project Cost
In-Resident Field Studies (50.0%)		
Cross-Cultural Aging Studies	8	$50,000
Rural Elderly	4	$50,000
Community Studies/ Intergenerational Ties	4	$35,000
Institutionalization	3	$35,000
Ethnic/Minority Aging	2	$35,000
Home/On-Site Interviewing (21.0%)		
Retirement Issues	5	$25,000

Older Women	3	$25,000
Oldest-Old	1	$25,000
Mailed Schedules (23.8%)		
Health Policy	4	$15,000
Advocacy Studies	2	$15,000
Medical Compliance	2	$15,000
Gerontology Education	1	$10,000
Volunteerism	1	$10,000
Analysis: Surveys, Census (4.7%)		
Regional/Local Inventories	2	$10,000

Note: Based on completed survey by twelve anthropologists, nineteen sociologists, and eleven social workers who completed the Ph.D. in their fields with a gerontology focus and are university associated.

participation in treatment planning, will ever be adequately clarified without extensive personal interviewing and behaviorally based research methods. Although social gerontologists thus evince a great diversity of interest in a range of potential research projects, their actual research funding requirements seem constrained. This is strikingly clear even though research results would significantly contribute to our knowledge of aging and the aging process in a variety of world contexts and on a diverse number of domestic policy fronts. Foundations should remember that their largesse has already encompassed a $100,000 gift for the establishment of social and recreational services at only one senior center, as well as a hefty $90,000 grant to support improvement in patient selection methods at a hospital devoted to the treatment of osteoarthritis. As worthy as these subventions are, their long-term effectiveness would seem to require a knowledge base that could help evaluate the adjustment of the elderly to newly designed programs. At the very least, patient selection for hospital treatment programs demands data on how the elderly of diverse backgrounds might perform with respect to illness presentation and medical compliance. The cultural molding of hospital usage patterns and treatment outcomes has long been known to be a conditioning factor in medical service delivery to youthful and midlife populations (Fabrega, 1971). A measured $15,000 grant could tell us how the cultural organization of aging would affect medical services to the elderly as well. This form of grant appears needed in the light of the large sums foundations are dispensing for elder care without, however, funding the type of empirical work that could lend health programming for older adults a needed sensitivity as well as a predictive value.

Government and foundation grant makers have favored biogerontology research or program supports for the elderly. Philanthropic organizations in particular have not seized the opportunity to sponsor studies on program evaluation or on the quality of service delivery to the elderly within institutional settings. In these contexts, empirical data on older adult behavior, life histories, or life-course materials, and culturological understandings could complement a biomedical approach to elder care and help to provide clinicians with more refined diagnoses and treatment plans. Such data ultimately require more than attitudinal surveys and information gained from archival sources. They demand extensive personal interviews and in many instances a period of local residence and participant-observation methods in order to clarify biomedical data in the light of social realities. Therefore, it would seem that increased foundation funding to the elderly or to social gerontology research might not mean better foundation grant making. Future foundation funding to social gerontology might take the direction of a conscious attempt to strengthen existent links between clinical gerontology and evaluative or policy-oriented social gerontology studies. As a well-known geriatric physician at a New York City hospital once remarked, "What good is it if we have clinical or recreational programs for older adults in outreach form, and little sense of how to involve them or their family members?"[5]

Foundation grant making for the elderly and scholarship in social gerontology nevertheless share three major features. Each has shown evidence of a sensitivity to place, program, and service delivery. Foundation support for research in social gerontology has a decidedly programmatic underpinning. Social gerontology has evolved its own prominent seeds of pragmatism and policy development that have often been related to the clinical aspects of service delivery to the elderly. Foundations and social gerontologists could now profit from this joint focus by wedding research in Aging Studies to the foundation penchant for project innovation, maintenance, and expansion. Dr. Wycliffe Rose's desire to "make the peaks higher" may have proved a problematic course for foundation activity in the case of graduate science education. Building on that which is already well established in foundation grant making for the elderly, however, is a worthy process and a healthy meeting ground for philanthropists and social gerontologists alike.

NOTES

1. Quoted in Kuhn (1977:179).
2. Quoted in ibid. (p. 183).
3. Quoted in Kevles (1987:293).
4. See Weiss and Mahlmann (1987).
5. Guido Celano, M.D., chief of the Geriatrics Section, Lincoln Hospital, New York City, and researcher on adult diabetes in a letter to the author.

7
Facing Age Neutrally

> Historians believe and justly resent the fact that sociologists make too many abstractions and separate unduly the various elements of society.
>
> Marcel Mauss (1923:78)

The relationship that foundations have enjoyed with social gerontologists has not been what the early twentieth-century anthropologist, Marcel Mauss, would have termed the "easiest or fastest" to effect. Nevertheless, foundations have shown a willingness to support programs for the American elderly and to provide a measured amount of monies for social gerontology research linked to evaluations of projects that provide the aged with a range of services. Moreover, an equally measured share of foundation subventions has gone to the type of social research in gerontology that shows a welcome indifference to program or pragmatism.

The social gerontology research reviewed in Chapter 6 represents a bare backbone of research interests in the field as these interests may be gleaned from the scientific journals. No real attention has been paid to studies that appear in book or in monograph form that reflect rich and diverse intellectual constituencies within social gerontology (Osgood and Sontz, 1989; Silverman, 1987). However, funding agencies need to know where research supports have originated and where they have not originated in order to develop a clarified view of their own role in social gerontology scholarship. Thus, information on research funding sources is today best derived from published articles rather than from books or monographs where more synthetic understandings tend to be presented without clear reference to monetary underpinnings. This lack of clear reference is often to the credit of a funding agency, for research supports must ultimately leave the texture of organized grant giving and assume a public life of their own. Such a process of selection nevertheless makes the archeology of philanthropy problematic and uncertain. That which has been recovered may be only partially reflective of endeavors in the field and therefore tends to remain unrepresentative of the philanthropic scope or spirit.

The term *social gerontology*, popularized by Clark Tibbets in the early 1960s, was meant to encompass that aspect of knowledge that deals with the linkages among aging, society, and culture and between the aging process and behavior (Osgood, 1989). Studies in social gerontology have thus exhibited a concern for the impact of social, cultural, and historical environments on the aging process and in the way the influence of these environments may differ from the effects of the biological processes of aging on the human organism. The social gerontology agenda is a flourishing one, and each facet of this agenda has developed its own scholarly lineage. However, it is not at all evident that research results presented in the scientific journals have as yet been phrased in predictive terms or propositions. As Nancy J. Osgood has emphasized, there is still no grand theorem that can provide an appropriate backdrop for social gerontology research or hypothesis testing. Rather, available conceptual frameworks underscore lower-level propositions about the social and cultural mechanisms that mediate adjustment to old age, social arrangements that help promote a sense of well-being in later life, and the influence of social forces on the aged's self-concept in particular historical and cultural contexts. Theories in social gerontology thus revolve around an integrationalist approach in the social sciences and social work; they also tend to favor theoretical and policy research that explores the way in which older adults can best maintain a full sense of participation in society in later life. A brief review of these theories appears warranted in the light of their relationship to scholarly and clinical work in social gerontology.

At least four major theoretical perspectives have guided social gerontology research in recent years. A "disengagement" perspective first suggested that healthy and independent older adults tended gradually to withdraw or distance themselves from social attachments in preparation for the ultimate disengagement, finality. This withdrawal was seen as adaptive for the individual, as well as functional for society, which could move smoothly to replenish vacant positions with more youthful populations (Cumming and Henry, 1961). Much research has arisen in counterpoint to disengagement theories. For example, it has been shown that many older adults do not show evidence of social withdrawal but rather remain active participants in society through ties to family members and associational attachments. Moreover, these "activity" theory perspectives have stressed that the level of morale among older adults rises with increased activity levels, especially in retirement communities or in settlements where age peers predominate (Osgood, 1989).

Another broad theory in social gerontology has drawn on analyses of societies that are divided by a series of age-grades through which individuals pass as they mature. Each age-grade is usually characterized by its own power to convey differential access to resources, alternate role relationships, and varying prerogatives associated with ritualistic conduct and behavior. Since every society exhibits some form of age-grading it has followed that the organization of age-grades will differ cross-culturally according to a variety of social, cultural, and historical conditions.

A final framework for social gerontology research has concerned the impact of processes of modernization on traditional or primitive societies. The growth of urbanization, literacy levels, and sophisticated health care systems has been correlated with heightened longevity. Modernization has also brought about a substantial decline in the level of personal and social deference behaviors to the elderly (Silverman and Maxwell, 1978). Additional theories have posited that declines in deference are due to pronounced imbalances in the nature of exchange relationships between young and old in modernizing situations (Osgood, 1989). During modernization, for example, the elderly suffer social losses stemming from retirement from positions of political and economic power. They also lack a modern education. The social valuables needed to engage in reciprocal transactions with midlife and younger adults are thus unavailable to the elderly, and their capacity to enter into egalitarian relationships with others is thereby curtailed.

Even in the face of much diversity, these prominent theoretical guides to social gerontology research nevertheless share similar outlooks and implications. Each conceptual framework is not tautly bound to any particular culture or society and can easily become part of the repertoire of the cross-national or cross-cultural analyst. The trend in social gerontology is toward uncovering what is universal to the aging process and toward understanding how sociocultural organizations may mediate the way in which this process is treated, experienced, and structured by the elderly and other members of a society. Social gerontologists therefore find analyses of modernization particularly significant. Though modernization is itself a worldwide phenomenon, it is far from complete within every society or subculture. Modernizing contexts thus provide a broad arena in which cross-cultural data on the elderly and the aging process can be tested.

Another common feature of social gerontology theories is that the aged are not regarded as an isolated group or separate population segment. Withdrawal from social attachments in an attempt to disengage implies that those who are withdrawing have enjoyed social attachments throughout the life span. Moreover, those older adults who may belong to a particular age-grade in society do not live separately from midlife and younger adults in other age-grades. Rather, older adults are linked to more youthful members of society through varied forms of kinship and associational ties. Further, a loss of some activities in later life does not always imply that other types of activities with family members and friends cannot be developed. To social gerontologists, therefore, *the aged are not merely an object of social science but of the science of society and of its integrative properties.* Indeed, much of the work foundations have already supported addresses itself to issues surrounding levels of morale in later life and the degree of older adult participation in institutional settings. The fact that current journal presentations tend to be based on attitudinal surveys does not at all demean the concept that older adults are intimately joined to the fabric of society. Such research serves only to question the way in which this integration can best be elucidated and underscores the need for research projects that are extended in time and behaviorally based.

A final common facet of social gerontology theories is that they can be flexibly oriented toward questions that embrace a number of clinical fields. If the elderly as a group do not undergo a process of disengagement, will some elderly individuals nevertheless withdraw as part of an adaptive process linked to illness and sick-role behaviors (Fabrega, 1971)? If morale is best gained in age-peer settings, is this also true for clinical situations? How, then, can clinicians best modify treatment environments in order to enhance positive age-peer influences without undermining family and community ties? These questions can be readily informed by social gerontology research and instruction, which stresses a need for the acquisition of a multidisciplinary knowledge base on the part of medical and health specialists. Often in contrast to other practitioners, clinical gerontologists view the elderly as inhabitating a rich sociocultural space characterized by a variety of social attachments. These attachments can be drawn upon in order to clarify diagnoses and treatment planning and in order to make the older adult a creative participant in the clinical situation (Maynard and Shiffman, 1988).

The principal conclusion to arise from this discussion of social gerontology theories is that there may be as many foundation entry points into social gerontology scholarship as there are research concepts or topics. Foundation support could contribute to a clarification of disengagement and activity theories or to the study of the elderly in modernizing contexts. Evaluative studies of clinical applications and hospital usage rates among the elderly of diverse cultural origin also seem warranted. A more indirect but equally probable entry point into the science of aging would be a foundation focus on general trends in gerontology education, faculty development within social gerontology, and the growth of gerontology instructional units in American university systems. To be sure, contemporary colleges no longer have the fly-by-night flavor of the early twentieth century when Carnegie and Rockefeller subventions were needed as a corrective for abuses in haphazard admissions policies and because of a striking lack of standardization in university curricula. Nor does the current academic landscape necessitate a strong foundation approach to the building of physical structures and libraries. Rather, foundation interventions for the purpose of supporting the evolution of social gerontology education require a more calculated and refined consciousness than organized philanthropy might have been able to produce in the first few decades of the century. More specifically, the foundation interest in term grant making might build upon two already existent research trends that are attempting to clarify the role of the study of aging in contemporary academic life. One of these trends seeks to define better the science of aging as a multidisciplinary field that contains both theoretical and clinical components. Another research direction is the resurrection of an older foundation concern for the quality of graduate medical education and speaks to the growing necessity of integrating sociocultural studies of the elderly into medical school curricula.

COLLECTIVITY AND COMMUNITY IN GERONTOLOGY EDUCATION

The science of aging is an interdisciplinary field that encompasses a special *collectivity*: a group of scholars of which social gerontologists constitute an important part. No real *community* of scholars as yet exists, for there is little agreement on common norms within the collectivity, nor is there a mutually agreed upon set of approaches or methods. Students of higher education might view social gerontology as defined largely by conceptual paradigms and therefore as a terminal branch of knowledge that contains data from many disciplines but is still not unified or "wholly single-tracked" (Weiss, 1966:170).

Distinct disciplines, including anthropology, sociology, and social work, have indeed framed foundation grant giving to early-twentieth-century institutions of higher learning. These grants, however, followed already emergent trends in academic social science and its development in university systems. Foundation trustees might have remembered Voltaire's statement that "God is always on the side of the heaviest battalions" (quoted in Selden, 1960:xv), for in the early days of foundation life, the academic battalions were plentiful but so ill defined and dispersed that Henry S. Pritchett, first president of the Carnegie Corporation, could declare that the term *college* or *university* had no "fixed meaning" (Selden, 1960:35). Having lent both university and departmental environments a lasting stability, foundation interventions into academic social gerontology today would seem less defined by a necessity for minimum standards and facilities than by an encounter with issues of academic examination, assessment, and experimentation.

The slow movement from collectivity to community in social gerontology has itself been accompanied by a series of questions regarding the process of discipline building. One primary question involves the issue of whether the science of aging should evolve as a distinct discipline or remain a focus of interest within established academic fields. Although there has been no final resolution of this question, some scholars feel that Aging Studies will soon see a growth of Ph.D.-awarding departments and associated interdisciplinary doctoral programs (Parhan and Wood, 1988). Foundation-sponsored research could clarify the movement from collectivity to community in the science of aging by uncovering methods, terminologies, and research goals that may be common to gerontology studies in all of the academic fields where the process of aging has attracted the interest of scholars.

Another question surrounding the growth of the science of aging in university systems is linked to its prominent clinical component. Should gerontology clinicians be licensed by a generic accrediting agency, or should licensure be left to the discretion of established academic disciplines and departments? In this instance, foundation work could support research designed to establish criteria against which individual competencies in health service delivery to the elderly might be assessed.

If the contemporary foundations will therefore not find the hodgepodge quality of an earlier academic context, they will nevertheless confront the challenge of clarifying a range of stimulating ideas linked to discipline building within the science of aging and to the academic specialization of a growing field of scholarly activity. These ideas need evaluation and study so that educational resources commensurate with a rising demand for social gerontology researchers and clinical gerontologists can be developed. Conference monies could be provided in order to bring together engaged educators, scientists, and practitioners for the purpose of assessing academic growth patterns and needs in the universities. Consensus panels attached to professional societies form a welcome basis for funding where guidelines for gerontology instruction can be evolved and agreed upon.

Trends in demography and academic growth clearly indicate that a research focus on aging and the aging process will not decline or disappear, only to be comfortably absorbed within established disciplines and departments. There has already been too much of a movement toward specialization in university systems and too lengthy a history of formal program development allied with undergraduate and graduate degrees. Questions of academic specialization and the legitimacy of licensure still needed to be addressed in a consistent manner. Creative foundation interventions may have a settling effect on the contemporary scientific impulse whose quickened pace seems familiar to that of the early twentieth century when foundation programming first began to link readily with university growth.

MEDICAL EDUCATION AND SOCIAL GERONTOLOGY

If foundations do not yet share rich relations with social gerontologists, ties between social gerontologists and specialists in geriatric medicine are even less defined. This remains true despite the fact that other practitioners, including experts in geriatric rehabilitation, have moved increasingly to a belief in the efficacy of multidisciplinary work in geriatric treatment (Maynard and Shiffman, 1988).

One way to gauge the professional distance between social gerontology and geriatrics, a subspecialty of medicine that focuses on the elderly, is to evaluate the degree to which the concerns of social gerontology have actually penetrated graduate medical contexts. A recent study reported that at least sixteen out of twenty-five medical colleges surveyed offered required courses in geriatric medicine (Sontz, 1986). (There are forty-five medical colleges in the continental United States.) However, none of these courses had been instituted before 1981. Another nine medical colleges offered elective course work in geriatrics that had also joined the medical curriculum only in recent years. Course work in anthropology, sociology, and social work was found at six of the medical schools surveyed; this course work had been instituted only on an elective basis. Geriatrics is, of course, a relatively recent subspecialty in medical education, but the limited accessibility to social gerontology understandings that American medical students now possess seems continuingly discouraging.

In particular, it seems difficult to believe that once having left the graduate schools of medicine, physicians will be able to acquire the type of multidisciplinary knowledge they will increasingly need in hospitals, nursing settings, and home health care situations where medical anthropologists, sociologists, and gerontological social workers will form a vital addition to biomedical applications. Foundations can easily and cost-effectively support the work of university geriatric education centers and other forums where discussions of the value of collaborations between medical practitioners and social gerontologists can be communicated to medical educators. Equally significant foundation initiatives in geriatric education can come in the form of supports to social gerontology researchers who are in a favorable position to study innovative ways in which to assimilate relevant social gerontology faculty and textual materials into academic medicine.

Only the University of Pennsylvania has managed to loosen traditional holds to the premedical requirement for admission into graduate medical faculties. Perhaps this great university has appropriately arrived at the conclusion that one does not need a premedical education in order to perform competently in graduate medical contexts or as a practitioner. This is not to say that graduate medical faculties should engage in a form of compensatory education for those who have pursued a liberal arts academic track or an immersion in history or the social sciences. But the likelihood of an undergraduate encounter with increasingly sophisticated and medically relevant social gerontology understandings is significantly decreased when specialization in biomedicine characterizes undergraduate study. If not all medical students will choose geriatrics as a postdoctoral specialization, the chance that their patient populations will become increasingly older is highly probable, if not inevitable. To walk triumphantly through the academic gates into the hospital or nursing setting without a corpus of advanced social gerontology knowledge is representative of a glaring gap in educational contexts that the great foundations helped to establish. This gap should be rectified. Medical students, our elderly, and the general public deserve no less.

CONCLUSIONS: OLD AGE IN THE LIFE OF AMERICAN FOUNDATIONS

Some of the earliest of American foundations are now approaching eighty years of age. Their development cannot easily be subdivided into critical phases, for there has been a continuity from youth to maturity in the foundation emphasis on funding for institutions of higher learning, supports for medical education, and subventions for epidemiological studies connected with the state of public health. Moreover, a change in the nature of trusteeship has not always prompted innovative funding designs. Rather, foundation funding constituencies have been largely delineated by foundation presidents who helped bring adult education and an interest in ethnicity to the Carnegie and to other larger foundations over the past two decades. In contrast, presidential changes at the Ford Foundation have brought about a desultory decline in International Studies in favor of a series of forays into Women's Studies that has continued on long after its principal advocates have disappeared from the law courts into the boardrooms and the community of diversified scholars. Whether there is agreement or disagreement with foundation priorities, these definite shifts in direction clearly indicate that the later life of the major foundations has not been characterized by stereotypical retreats into mental rigidity or an incapacity to adapt to changing social conditions. As institutions, foundations have retained their intellectual plasticity. What matters, therefore, is not whether this flexibility still exists but the extent to which both intellectual adaptability and generosity can continue to intervene effectively in critical societal problems. It is the case today, as it was yesterday, that such institutional flexibility has the power to provoke a justifiable tendency for outsiders to review foundation priorities and to raise questions surrounding the public accountability of the philanthropic trusts.

Given our rising population of older adults and the widespread distribution of demographic studies attesting to this growth, there are few foundations that have established anything more than indifferent liaisons with pressing issues of aging in society. A brief survey of foundation contributions might serve to clarify a few of the reasons why this linkage remains underdeveloped. Any such review should begin with the ability to place science patronage on a sustained and sure footing in the early twentieth century. This relative funding stability permitted early research in the sciences of humankind to occur at appropriate and often distant geographic sites and helped move scholars out of the overly speculative academic armchair. Subventions to undergraduate and graduate education also remodeled scientific philanthropy so that it could assume the professional status it enjoys today. Most important, foundations foresaw that the social sciences had predictive capabilities and could thus add vitally to social policies in a way that ultimately hindered distinctions between the disadvantaged and those who thought it a "disgrace to die rich." The provision of an opportunity to advance personally and economically through academic achievement was, in an era of federal indifference to higher education, largely a consequence of foundation grant giving.

The early years of the great foundations also offered a surfeit of research problems associated with industrialization and massive immigration. These were problems of such magnitude that the "no-policy" stance of the philanthropic trusts was accompanied by a type of modern system thinking—a concern for the specifics of research without, however, overlooking the results of research in elucidating broad societal questions. In those days, the aged remained a largely rural population and decidedly invisible to a foundation benevolence that was urban oriented and entailed the grander designs of university development and academic growth. The study of the aged and the aging process was thus left to enter scholarly research agendas in a cautious, modest, and random way.

A related foundation contribution has been gradually to refashion the concept of disadvantaged Americans for purposes of grant making and service delivery. Original foundation donors were intent on promoting the "greatest good for the greatest number." This was obviously a rather unspecific ideology as far as the content of actual programming was concerned, yet it was well delineated insofar as the "greatest number" ultimately referred to the poor and disadvantaged. Slowly, for the purpose of more clearly targeting foundation supports, the great endowments began to divide Americans into distinct groups based on ethnicity, race, immigrant background, gender, and even age. This philanthropic focus on the social minority has had a number of advantages. It has meant that the foundation network has expanded to include those with economic resiliency who have nevertheless suffered from various forms of discrimination. To a smaller extent, the foundation use of the social minority as a modern repository of the foundation burden has also provoked a measured attention to the elderly and to research on aging. Whether the fragmentation of society for foundation purposes will actually produce the greatest good for the most Americans may be a question best answered by future analysts. Still another question, however, may be immediately posed and responded to: Will the foundation view of the elderly as yet another social minority turn out to be beneficial for older adults, or will this aspect of foundation strategizing prove inappropriate to the needs and welfare of the aged?

First, it seems clear that the elderly cannot be considered a monolithic group. Not all older adults are disadvantaged in an economic sense. Moreover, many older adults maintain high levels of political and economic activity. Equally noteworthy is that few among the elderly would want to be included in a distinct group for foundation granting purposes solely because of their age. Indeed, only a small number of older adults actually see themselves as being old, especially if they are reasonably healthy and socially engaged with family members and friends of various ages. While according the elderly a separate status in society might act to heighten a sense of identification with other older adults, this same sense of common identity might also serve to undermine supportive attachments with more youthful populations. Foundations, in short, need to emphasize the ties that bind the elderly to others in society rather than evolve a grantgiving pattern that focuses solely on those properties that may characterize the elderly as members of a distinctive social group.

Second, social gerontology research does not seem to favor approaches that would underscore the aged's position as an American social minority. Disengagement theories have always been accompanied by those that stress attachment to members of other age groups. Theories that stress aging in relation to the rest of society and to its varied organizations, groupings, and associations are ultimately oriented toward defining the universalities of the aging process amid social and cultural diversity. Such theories are not overly inclined to view the elderly as a separate group that needs still further definition as a specific population unit. For this reason, social gerontologists have a desire to clarify when age, ethnicity, income, and gender are consistent mediators of behavior and when they are of only situational value to the elderly and to practitioners (Cool, 1987). Further, social gerontologists have begun to note that policies directed solely to aged constituencies may be too compartmentalizing and may act to negate relationships with the young or perpetuate negative stereotypes about the elderly that have already been present in society for too long a time (Lowy, 1988).[1] Policies that are inclusive of everyone's needs, or *age-neutral* policies, complement the social gerontologist's desire to uncover the commonalities of human behavior through the study of later life and do not lead inexorably toward the social separation of the elderly from other populations or toward their definition as a distinct social minority.

Even with these caveats in mind, it still does not seem beyond the power of many American foundations to recognize the dramatic growth in our older adult population and to respond creatively to this growth by supporting scientific investigations in the field of social gerontology. The philanthropic trusts might continue their traditional interest in higher education and fund studies of departmental growth in gerontology, curriculum planning for future researchers and clinicians, and issues concerning professional licensure. Medical education is in real need of catching up with understandings of human behavior derived from the social sciences and from social work. The necessity of examining the quality of medical education is not as compelling today as it was when Abraham Flexner and the Carnegie Foundation undertook their highly critical assessment in the early part of the century (Wallis, 1966:48). However, there are still far too many graduate medical students who read little more during a semester than mimeographed professorial notes. Their elders have deftly helped them to avoid the intellectual rigors of interdisciplinary research papers and effectively denied them exposure to ideas that indicate that illness presentation and treatment outcomes may be socially and culturally defined. Increasingly medical students will require an analytic and humanistic thrust to their education—not only because this type of education will make them better health practitioners but also because a growingly sophisticated public demands sensitive interactions with modern service deliverers and other craftsmen. Educational research by social gerontologists can become a welcome focus of foundation activity in this regard, for many have already linked sociocultural theory with clinical situations. They are thus in a crucial position to help close what remains an outstanding gap in the sharing of biomedical and social scientific understandings.

Even a modest foundation can thus build social gerontology research into its grant making for the elderly. This grant giving has been largely pragmatic and has not undertaken the risk-taking movement toward delicate affiliations with the future that was a characteristic of the early foundation climate. It is possible that foundation inattention to social gerontology derives from the fact that pragmatic programs for American social minorities have become too convenient and valuable an arena for the relief of the foundation burden. It is also possible that the social sciences may appear too problematic an investment for some contemporary foundation stewards; theoretical findings from emergent fields are dissimilar to the measurable outcomes of projects and are therefore not as likely to provoke feelings of institutional gratification (Morison, 1966:100).

Yet a cursory review of early foundation activities clearly indicates that these were not only specific and pragmatic in outlook but rather devoted considerable attention to broad and trenchant questions about the nature and functioning of society and of the foundations' role within it. Disadvantaged status was seen as both a relative and comparative concept that had a historical depth and a palpable future in any civilization. To foundation trustees, the reform of educational systems appeared an artifact of a society's need to replenish itself over the long term. Foundation efforts at reconstruction following periods of devastating conflict were considered as "demonstration work" and could be replicated and refined in other relief systems throughout the world.

Human aging is a phenomenon that penetrates the total fabric of society as well. The science of aging invites the philanthropic foundations to confront cross-national similarities and differences in the aging process, problems of succession to high office, issues concerning intergenerational ties, and a health service delivery system linked to all people, some of whom happen to be older than others. This invitation comes none too soon. It addresses a more ancient philanthropic mandate to act not only in response to the immediate context but also in anticipation of the future.

NOTE

1. Lowy (1989:29–30) has pointed out the advantages of policies for the elderly that can address their specific needs. There is, however, a tendency for such policies to isolate the elderly for purposes of service delivery. Lowy suggests that social services to the elderly include younger and midlife adults.

Appendix: National Foundations Giving Grants to Social Gerontology Research

National foundations are those that have no local or regional restrictions in grant making. Policy research as well as studies of gerontological education may also be funded by these organizations.

Alcoa Foundation, 1501 Alcoa Building, Pittsburgh, Pennsylvania 15219.

Florence V. Burden Foundation, 630 Fifth Avenue, Suite 2900, New York, New York 10111.

Commonwealth Fund, 1 East Seventy-fifth Street, New York, New York 10021.

Educational Foundation of America, 35 Church Lane, Westport, Connecticut 06880.

Paul F. Glenn Foundation, 72 Virginia Drive, Manhasset, New York 11030.

MacArthur Foundation, 140 South Dearborn Street, Chicago, Illinois 60603.

Milbank Memorial Fund, 1 East Seventy-fifth Street, New York, New York 10021.

APPENDIX

Pew Memorial Trust, c/o Glenmede Trust Company, 229 South Eighteenth Street, Philadelphia, Pennsylvania 19103.

Retirement Research Foundation, 325 Touhy Avenue, Park Ridge, Illinois 60068.

Villers Foundation, 1334 G Street N.W., Washington, D.C. 20005.

Selected Bibliography

Achenbaum, W. A. 1978. *Old Age in the New Land: The American Experience since 1790.* Baltimore and London.
Administration on Aging. 1982. *Grants to Research on Aging, 1979–1981.* Washington, D.C.
Andrews, F. E. 1950. *Philanthropic Giving.* New York.
———. 1956. *Philanthropic Foundations.* New York.
Angell, J. 1931. *President's Message: 1921.* Carnegie Corporation Bound Volume of Annual Reports. New York.
Arensberg, C. M., and S. T. Kimball. 1968. *Family and Community in Ireland.* Cambridge, Mass.
Barber, B. 1952. *Science and the Social Order.* New York.
Buechler, H., and J. M. Buechler, eds. 1987. *Migrants in Europe.* Westport, Conn.
Burgess, E. W., and D. J. Bogue. 1964. "Research in Urban Society." In *Urban Sociology,* edited by E. W. Burgess and D. J. Bogue. Chicago and London, pp. 1–15.
Cattell, J. 1927. "Origin and Distribution of Scientific Men." *Science* 66:513–516.
Codere, H. 1966. Introduction to *The Kwakiutl Indians,* by Franz Boas. New York.

Commager, H. S. 1950. *The American Mind*. New Haven and London.
Cool, L. E. 1987. "The Effects of Social Class and Ethnicity on the Aging Process." In *The Elderly as Modern Pioneers*, edited by P. Silverman. Bloomington and Indianapolis, pp. 263–282.
Crothers, S. 1911. "The Art of Philanthropy." *Charity* 14:1872–1905.
Cumming, E., and W. E. Henry. 1961. *Growing Old*. New York.
D'Andrade, R. G. et al. 1975. "Academic Opportunity in Anthropology." *American Anthropologist* 77(4):753–773.
Darnell, R. 1977. "History of Anthropology in Historical Perspective." *Annual Review of Anthropology* 6:399–417.
Devine, E. T. 1904. "Some Elementary Definitions of Charity." *Charity* 12:595–602.
———. 1906. "Dominant Note of Modern Philanthropy." *Charity* 16:340–345.
Donaldson, H. H. 1904. "Endowed Research." *Outlook* 78:1012–1013.
———. 1906. "Some Aspects of the Endowment of Research." *Science* 23:282–286.
Eggan, F. 1968. "One Hundred Years of Ethnology and Social Anthropology." In *One Hundred Years of Anthropology*, edited by J. Brew. Cambridge, Mass., pp. 119–152.
Fabrega, H. Jr. 1971. "Medical Anthropology." In *Biennial Review of Anthropology*, edited by B. Siegel. Stanford, pp. 167–229.
Flexner, A. 1915a. *Funds and Foundations*. New York.
———. 1915b. "Is Social Work a Profession?" *School and Society* 1:901–911.
Fosdick, R. B. 1964. *Adventure in Giving: The Story of the General Education Board*. New York and Evanston.
George, M. 1986. *The Autobiography of Henry VIII*. New York.
Gettleman, M. E. 1979. *An Elusive Presence: The Discovery of John H. Finley and His America*. Baltimore.
Gilman, D. C. 1907. "Five Great Gifts." *Outlook* 86:648–657.
Gould, R., D. Koster, and A. H. L. Sontz. "The Lithic Assemblage of the Western Desert Aborigines of Australia." *American Antiquity* 36(2):149–169.

Hall, P. D. 1984. *The Organization of American Culture, 1700–1900*. New York.
Harrar, J. G. 1964. Foreword to R. B. Fosdick, *Adventure in Aging: The Story of the General Education Board*. New York and Evanston, pp. vii–viii.
Harris, M. 1968. *The Rise of Anthropological Theory: A History of Theories of Culture*. New York.
Henderson, C. 1900. "Science in Philanthropy." *Atlantic* 85:249–254.
Hornum, B., and A. P. Glascock. 1989. "Whither Anthropological Gerontology?" In *The Science and Practice of Gerontology*, edited by N. J. Osgood and A. H. L. Sontz. Westport, Conn.
Kalosieh, R. A., and J. P. Pedoto. 1989. "Counseling in Gerontology: Perspectives from Counseling Psychology." In *The Science and Practice of Gerontology*, edited by N. J. Osgood and A. H. L. Sontz. Westport, Conn.
Keith, J. 1982. *Old People as People: Social and Cultural Influences on Aging and Old Age*. Boston.
Kevles, D. J. 1987. Orig. 1971. *The Physicists: The History of a Scientific Community in Modern America*. Cambridge, Mass.
Kuhn, T. 1977. Orig. 1961. "The Function of Measurement in Modern Physical Science." In *The Essential Tension*, edited by T. Kuhn. Chicago and London, pp. 178–224.
Kuklick, H. 1973. "A Scientific Review: Social Theory in the United States: 1930–1945." *Social Inquiry* 43:3–22.
Larson, M. S. 1977. *The Rise of Professionalism: A Sociological Analysis*. Berkeley.
Lattimore, A. 1909. "The New Philanthropy." *Outlook* 93:593–596.
Lopata, H. A. 1964. "The Function of Voluntary Associations in an Ethnic Community: Polonia." In *Urban Sociology*, edited by E. W. Burgess and D. J. Bogue. Chicago and London, pp. 117–137.
Lowy, L. 1989. "Current Trends in the Theory, Research and Practice of Social Work with the Aged." In *The Science and Practice of Gerontology*, edited by N. J. Osgood and A. H. L. Sontz. Westport, Conn.

Lubove, R. 1974. *Professional Altruists: The Emergence of Social Work as a Career: 1880-1930*. New York.
McCaughey, R. 1984. *International Studies and Academic Enterprise: A Chapter in the Enclosure of American Learning*. New York.
Mauss, M. 1923. *The Gift*. New York.
Maynard, M., and L. Shiffman. 1988. "Geriatric Rehabilitation." Manuscript. Virginia Commonwealth University/Virginia Medical College.
Mendelsohn, E. 1966. Introduction to *The Golden Age of Science*, edited by B. Jones. New York.
Merton, R. 1973. *The Sociology of Science*. New York.
Miller, H. 1970. *Dollars for Research*. Seattle, Washington.
Moore, J., and J. Birren. 1971. "Doctoral Training in Gerontology." *Journal of Gerontology* 26:249-257.
Morison, R. 1966. "Foundations and Universities." In *The Contemporary University*, edited by R. Morison. Boston, pp. 75-109.
National Institutes of Health. 1986. *National Institute on Aging: Seventh Report of Council on Program, October, 1985*. Bethesda, Md.
―――. 1987. *The Search for Health*. Bethesda, Md.
Nee, D. M., and D. M. Bracco. 1986. *Grantmaking for the Elderly: An Analysis of Foundation Expenditures, 1978-1982*. New York.
Newcomb, S. 1900. "Science and the Government." *North American Review* 170:666-678.
―――. 1902. "Conditions That Discourage Scientific Work in America." *North American Review* 174:145-158.
Nielson, W. A. 1972. *The Big Foundations*. New York.
Osgood, N. J. 1989. "Theory and Research in Social Gerontology." In *The Science and Practice of Gerontology*, edited by N. J. Osgood and A. H. L. Sontz. Westport, Conn.
―――, and A. H. L. Sontz, eds. 1989. *The Science and Practice of Gerontology*. Westport, Conn.
Owen, D. 1964. *English Philanthropy: 1660-1960*. Cambridge, Mass.
Parhan, I., and J. Wood. 1988. "The Beginnings of Educational Gerontology." Working paper. Department of Gerontology.

Virginia Commonwealth University/Virginia Medical College.
Parsons, E. Clews. 1900. "Fieldwork in Teaching Sociology." *Educational Review* 20:159–169.
Peterson, D. A. 1986. *Extent of Gerontology Instruction in American Institutions of Higher Learning*. Andrus Gerontology Center. University of Southern California.
_____. 1986–1987. *Organizational Structures of Gerontology Instructional Programs*. Andrus Gerontology Center. University of Southern California.
_____. 1987. *Gerontology Credentials*. Andrus Gerontology Center. University of Southern California.
Polansky, N., ed. 1975. *Social Work Research: Methods for the Helping Profession*. Chicago.
Rossi, P. 1966. "Researchers, Scholars and Policy Makers." In *The Contemporary University*, edited by R. Morison. Boston, pp. 110–129.
Selden, W. K. 1960. *Accreditation: The Struggle for Standards in Higher Education*. New York.
Shils, E. 1970. "Tradition, Ecology and Institution in the History of Sociology." *Daedalus* (Fall):760–825.
Silverman, P., ed. 1987. *The Elderly as Modern Pioneers*. Bloomington and Indianapolis.
Silverman, P., and R. J. Maxwell. 1978. "How Do I Respect Thee? Let Me Count the Ways: Deference towards Elderly Men and Women." *Behavior Science Research* 13(2):91–108.
Simmons, L. 1945. *The Role of the Aged in Primitive Society*. New Haven.
Sommer, J. 1987. "Mapping Federal Funding." *American Scientist* 75:447–448.
Sontz, A. H. L. 1986. *Medical Education and Gerontology*. New Brunswick, N.J.
Stimpson, C. R., and N. K. Cobb. 1986. *Women's Studies in the United States: A Report to the Ford Foundation*. New York.
Stocking. G. W. 1976a. "Ideas and Institutions in American Anthropology." In *Selected Papers from the American Anthropologist: 1921–1945*, edited by G. W. Stocking. Washington, D.C., pp. 1–54.

———, ed. 1976b. *Selected Papers from the American Anthropologist: 1921–1945*. Washington, D.C.

Sullivan, E., ed. 1985. *National Directory of Educational Programs in Gerontology*. 3d ed. Washington, D.C.

Trattner, W. I. 1974. *From Poor Law to Welfare State: A History of Social Welfare in America*. New York.

Tucker, F. 1905. "Social Stewardship: Duties of Governing Boards." *Charities* 15:291–295.

Wallis, W. A. 1966. "Centripetal and Centrifugal Forces in University Organization." In *The Contemporary University*, edited by R. Morison. Boston, pp. 39–50.

Weeks, E. 1966. *The Lowell Institute*. New York.

Weiss, D. M., and D. E. Mahlmann, comp. 1987. *National Guide to Funding in Aging*. New York.

Weiss, P. 1966. "Science in the University." In *The Contemporary University*, edited by R. Morison. Boston, pp. 152–185.

Wines, F. H. 1898. "Sociology and Philanthropy." *Annals of the American Academy* 12:49–57.

Young, R. M. 1966. "Scholarship in the History of the Behavioral Sciences." In *History of Science: An Annual Review of Literature, Research and Teaching*. Cambridge, England, 5:1–51.

Zuckerman, H. 1977. *Scientific Elite: Nobel Laureates in the United States*. New York.

Index

Administration on Aging, 91, 97–98
Anthropology, 39–40, 43–44, 47; Ph.D. productivity in Aging Studies, 61–63; postdoctoral research in Aging Studies, 75–76
Astronomy, philanthropic funding for, 5–6

Barnard College, 40–41. See also Parsons, Elsie Clews
Benevolent societies, 3
Biogerontology, xxii; federal funding for, 91; foundation funding for, 94
Boaz, Franz, 9–10

Carnegie, Andrew, 17
Carnegie Corporation, xx, 18, 33; and university reform, 30–31. See also Education
Charitable trusts, legal limitations on development, 2–3
Charity Organization Movement, xix, 39, 50
Chicago University, 7–9; and urban sociology, 8–9, 36–37, 44
Columbia University, 3, 9, 15
Commonwealth Fund, 32

Education: and the Carnegie Corporation, 26–27, 120; foundation grants to, 25–26

Ford Foundation, 66, 87
Foundations: classical, xix; grants to Aging Studies, 57,

Foundations (*continued*) 67, 92–97, 105; trusteeship in, 13, 20–25. *See also* Older adults

General Education Board, 18, 27–28
Gerontology: clinical, 111; instruction in, 79–85; licensing in, 113; in medical education, 114–116, 120; need for faculty in, 81–88. *See also* Social gerontology

Harvard University, 3, 5

International Studies, 66–67, 87

Laura Spelman Rockefeller Memorial Foundation, 15–16, 18, 28. *See also* Chicago University

Milbank Memorial Fund, 30

National Institute on Aging, 90–91, 98
National Institutes on Health, 57, 90–91, 98
National Research Council, 10, 15, 40
National Science Foundation, xxiv, 46, 98

Older adults: in American demography, xxi; and early-20th-century foundations, 52–53; and rural life, 53–55; as a social minority, 33, 118–119

Parsons, Elsie Clews: and philanthropy, 41; professional activities, 35, 40–42
Psychogerontology, xxii, xxv–xxvi

Rockefeller Foundation, xx, 29–30, 32, 35
Russell Sage Foundation, xx, 14, 31

Scientific philanthropy, 13, 37, 45
Smithsonian Institution, 5
Sociology, 44; Ph.D. productivity in Aging Studies, 61–63; postdoctoral research in social gerontology, 75–76
Social gerontology, xxii, 108; Ph.D. productivity in, 58–60; Ph.D. topics in, 66; policy in, 119, 121; postdoctoral research in, 74–79, 97–99, 102–104; theories in, 108–111
Social work, 14–15, 38–39; Freudian psychology in, 45; Ph.D. productivity in Aging Studies, 61–63; postdoctoral research in Aging Studies, 75–76; research in, 46

Wieboldt Foundation, 44
Women's Studies, 86–87

ABOUT THE AUTHOR

ANN H. L. SONTZ is an honors graduate of Barnard College and holds a Ph.D. in anthropology from Columbia University where she occupied a John W. Burgess Distinguished Fellowship. Dr. Sontz has written on three-generation immigrant families within the European Economic Community and on older immigrants in American small business enterprise. With Nancy J. Osgood, she recently coedited *The Science and Practice of Gerontology* (Greenwood Press).

Dr. Sontz is the founding president of the Brunswick Institute, a foundation that undertakes grant giving and research on science and science education in the fields of gerontology and human development. For several years she has been president of the Community Advisory Board of the Educational Opportunity Fund at Hudson County Community College in New Jersey, a governmental program for minorities, women, and older adults.